D1591706

A COLLECTOR'S GUIDE TO

BLACK GLASS

By MARLENA TOOHEY

Edited by TOM KLOPP

Table of Contents

Published by
ANTIQUE PUBLICATIONS
Marietta, Ohio 45750

ISBN: 0-915410-47-8 Softbound
0-915410-48-6 Hardbound

Index of Glass by Manufacturers

I started my collection of black glass over 20 years ago. It began with a 24-piece luncheon set. I had no idea it would turn into such a habit forming hobby.

It has been quite a learning experience for me putting this book together. I think you will find the knowledge and information included in this book will not only be useful as a reference but also quite interesting.

If you have any information about any of the pieces shown or any others you may have, please write me in care of Antique Publications. I would love hearing from you.

Marlena Toohey

Dedication

My loving thanks to my parents, John and Naomi Over, for all their help and support over the years.

Also to my husband John, and my sons Brian and Brandon, whose patience and understanding were especially great over the last 10 weeks of putting this book together!

Acknowledgement

My special thanks to the staff of Richardson Printing for all their help.

FOREWORD

One summer vacation my parents and I found ourselves hunting for antique shops in South Dakota. We came upon a small garage with an 'ANTIQUES' sign hanging over the front door. Naturally we stopped and went in. I was amazed at the amount of items one small garage could hold! There was shelf after shelf of everything you could ever imagine, and some things you couldn't imagine.

Being just 13, I wasn't really looking for any particular thing. I came upon some dishes that were six-sided and black. What a strange dish, I thought, and who ever would have thought of black dishes. Then I noticed the beautiful hand cut crystal stemware sitting beside them. It had black bases to match.

Just about that time, the owner of the shop, an elderly gentleman, walked up to me and said he wanted to show me something special about those dishes. He took me over to the window, where the sunlight was pouring in, and told me to look through the black dish. It was a beautiful deep purple. I had to check each piece to see if it was the same.

After I stood there for a while, the owner came back to me. He said, "Tell your old man you need $10.00 and you can have the whole set." That's where it all began! One small set of dishes, 22 pieces in all. As we finished our trip, we were amazed to see how many pieces of black glass we found.

Not knowing what I was getting myself into, I began picking up pieces at garage sales and flea markets. My mother and father, needless to say, ended up picking up the bills for my so-called hobby until I was older and started to work. It was exciting to have my own money, and wonder what piece I would find next. Within four years, my hobby had turned into a rather nice collection.

Then, having at least 1,000 pieces, I was sure I had one of everything, but it never seemed to end. A friend sent me a picture postcard from the Pioneer Museum in Mindon, Nebraska. It was a picture of what was said to be the largest black glass collection in the United States. How exciting it was to know that I already had all but a few of the pieces shown and about 800 that weren't! At that point, I think my collection turned into an obsession!

Even after 21 years, and 2,500 pieces, I'm still finding pieces I have never seen before. I still enjoy remembering where I purchased my pieces, and laugh at the prices I used to pay. Prices I may have thought to be ridiculously high then, I would love to pay for the same items now. I have found out that you don't have to know who made a piece to know that you like it. I have bought it because it was black.

I hope this book will help you whether you are a collector or a dealer. I have certainly enjoyed collecting the glass shown, and putting it all together for you. If you have any information or thoughts you would like to share, I would really enjoy hearing from you.

Happy Collecting!

INTRODUCTORY NOTE

Throughout the descriptions of the color section, the manufacturer's pattern name or number has been used where known. Where a name given by a writer of later years is used, it is followed by an asterisk (*) the first time it appears in the description of each color page.

An effort has also been made to use the manufacturers' item designations, as bowl, comport, jug, etc., when this information is available.

Dates given are, as far as possible, based on the available information for the exact item shown, and so may differ from those of other items in the same pattern. If the item is known to have been advertised in black in a particular year or years, it is dated accordingly. If the date when it was made in black is not known, the years when it is known to have been made are used, modified in some cases by the known period when its manufacturer made black glass. Because complete production records are seldom available, some items were undoubtedly made also in other years which could not be documented.

In the section "References by Figure Number" are listed the sources of the information presented on each item, and often where further details can be found. It has been attempted in this section to provide a comprehensive list of the books which discuss each item. Consequently there will occasionally be found a reference which presents information contrary to that in this book, as well as those which support it. Books designed primarily as price guides usually have not been cited, nor have periodicals, except where they provide information not found elsewhere.

Some of the books cited in this book are referred to simply by the author's name, followed by the volume number in case of a multi-volume work. Arbitrary abbreviations are used for some others; a key to these, as well as a full list of the works cited, is given in the Bibliography.

The History of Black Glass

The black glass covered in this book was made chiefly in the United States in this century. In the case of nearly every piece shown, the maker chose black for its decorative properties. However, through most of its history, black glass was used primarily for plain utilitarian items.

In centuries past, most common bottle glass was composed principally or entirely of sand and wood ashes. Due to the presence of iron and other impurities in these as used for this purpose, the glass usually assumed a green or amber color, these varying through many hues and depths. An increase in the proportion of wood ashes seems to have been all that was necessary in some cases to make the color so dark as to be practically opaque black. Other coloring agents were, however, sometimes employed.

In the mid-1600's, black glass was adopted in England for wine bottles, the purpose being to protect the contents from light. Black bottles were also regarded as tougher than others, a property especially important in containers for liquids which would ferment and build up pressure. For these reasons, black bottles came to be preferred for beverages such as beer, ale, and cider, as well as wine. This situation continued in the United States into the latter half of the nineteenth century. Those who wish to pursue further the history of black bottles before 1900 will find valuable information in *American Bottles and Flasks and Their Ancestry* by McKearin and Wilson. While none of these bottles are illustrated in the present book, one of the other types of household items freeblown in bottle factories in the same period is shown in Figure 422.

Black glass is said to have been used in some of the ornamental vessels made in the glass making center Venice in the centuries when it was an independent country, that is, before 1797. Not having investigated this field in depth, I am unable to present reliable details.

In the first half of the nineteenth century, some efforts to use black glass ornamentally were made elsewhere in Europe. It has been reported that a factory at Zechlin, north of Berlin, from 1804 made black glass items imitating the black basalt made in England. No illustrations or specific descriptions of these German pieces have come to my attention at this writing. The English black pottery was popular in tea sets, usually with embossed decoration.

In the catalogue of the Corning Museum's 1981 exhibition, *Czechoslovakian Glass 1350-1980*, can be seen three elegant and striking examples of black "hyalith" glass with gold decoration. Hyalith is identified as certain opaque red and opaque black glass, the black originated about 1817 in a Southern Bohemian glass works of one Count Buquoy, but made also at other factories. Two drinking vessels exhibited are finely decorated with oriental figures in a combination of bright and matte gold.

What we know as pressed glass was introduced in the 1820's, and gained wide popularity during the next decade. In France especially, it was developed in the 1830's in intricate embossed designs with stippled or similarly detailed backgrounds, called "lacy" by collectors. (Some pieces may actually have been mold-blown with the aid of a mechanical pump.) While glass in this style was made for many years in Europe, little appears to have been made in black; however, a black goblet in the Corning Museum of Glass is thought to have been made in France in the 1830's. The reader who wishes to investigate this field further will find only scattered references in English, but some assistance may be had from Innes, Spillman, Lee *(Sandwich Glass)*, and Heacock and Johnson (see Bibliography).

In the last quarter of the nineteenth century, several English manufacturers pressed novelties and tableware items of black (see Figures 341 and 350). Notable among these makers was the long-lived firm known in this period as Sowerby and Company, 1874-1882, and from 1882 on as Sowerby's Ellison Glass Works, Limited (Figure 461). Its factory at Gateshead-on-Tyne was reported in 1882 to be "the largest pressed glass manufactory in the world", producing "about 150 tons per week" of finished glassware. Some English firms embossed trademarks in their pressed glass; these were heraldic devices, Sowerby's being a peacock's head. Lattimore's *English 19th-Century Press-Moulded Glass* provides histories of principal manufacturers, as does, on a smaller scale, Godden's *Antique Glass and China*. Some hand-blown decorative items in black were also made in England in the late 1800's; a few examples of these, and of pressed items, are shown by Manley.

In the United States, black glass was little used for tableware or any items other than bottles in the nineteenth century, but scattered instances can be cited.

In the type of patterned mold-blown glass now known as blown three mold, a few shapes, including inkwells and tumblers, were occasionally made of black glass. Some of these items are said to have come from the factory on Marlboro Street in Keene, New Hampshire, probably while under the ownership of Justus Perry (1817-1822). Others were evidently made at the factory in Mt. Pleasant (near Saratoga Springs), New York, established by the Granger family in 1844. The principal published study of blown three mold wares is in McKearins' *American Glass*.

The earliest piece of black glass *pressed* in this country may have been a 3½″ cup plate in an imitation-cut design. This design, #46 in Lee and Rose's *American Glass Cup Plates*, is believed to have been made somewhere in the East Coast area from New England to Philadelphia, in the late 1820's and 1830's. Also known in black is #242-A, a cup plate in a lacy design including several flowers, made in the same section probably in the 1830's. Again, however, it is not possible to name the particular manufacturer responsible. Black examples of each of these plates were considered extremely rare by Lee and Rose, though each is much more available in clear glass and known in other colors. Both designs are pictured by the above authors. A black #46 is owned by The Corning Museum of Glass, and a photograph of it may be seen in Spillman's catalogue of the Museum's pressed glass.

Another lacy item rarely found in black is a rectangular salt dish, 2⅞″ long, MV 1 in the Neals' *Pressed Glass Salt Dishes of the Lacy Period*. This design comes in clear glass and various colors. Black (dense green and amber) examples have been attributed to the Mount Pleasant, New York, factory already mentioned. No doubt they were made there, after 1844; however, those in clear glass and at least some of those in other colors were made elsewhere, before that date.

Another rarity which deserves mention was probably made before 1850 in the area of Pittsburgh or of Wheeling, Virginia (now West Virginia). This is a 7½″ oval dish pressed in a bold all-over design combining elements borrowed from cut glass with stippling, in "very dark green glass appearing black in reflected light". The only example known in this color, also now at Corning, is illustrated on plate 146 of McKearins' *American Glass*.

Next we encounter the small covered jars in the shape of a bear sitting upright, muzzled, as shown on page 98 of Munsey's *Collecting Bottles*. These are recorded in four sizes, and various colors, including black. They are said to have held ointment or pomade. Some are embossed with the name of R. & G. A. Wright, Philadephia, who presumably sold such products packed in the jars; possibly other firms' names may be found. The jars themselves have been attributed to the Boston and Sandwich Glass Company, of Sandwich, Massachusetts, because of fragments found there. The period of their manufacture is approximately indicated by a nearly identical jar in pottery, marked to indicate that its design was registered in England in 1854.

Deming Jarves, prominently associated with the Boston and Sandwich Glass Company from its founding in 1825, left that organization in 1858. In the 1865 edition of his book *Reminiscences of Glass-Making*, he included two formulas for black glass. These may not have been original with Mr. Jarves, who merely stated that they "have with success been used". It will be noted that he did not itemize the basic ingredients such as sand, but only those added to produce the color:

To 1400 lbs. of batch add
    180 lbs. manganese,
    100 lbs. calcined iron scales, made fine,
     20 lbs. powdered charcoal,
     10 lbs. arsenic.

The second, being a flint (lead) glass, clearly was intended for fine wares:

    600 lbs. flint batch,
     40 lbs. manganese,
     46 lbs. oxide of iron.

A large group of formulas hand-written in a notebook evidently used at the Boston and Sandwich Glass Company about 1859-1865 also includes black.

Around this time, the items pressed of black glass were probably most often bases of kerosene lamps. These were usually attached by metal connectors to fonts of clear or contrasting colored glass; examples may be seen in Thuro's *Oil Lamps II*. Enough varieties of these lamps, appearing to be from the 1860's, have been found to indicate that a number of manufacturers were involved, but most cannot be named. An exception is the Pittsburgh firm of M'Kee and Brothers, whose 1864 illustrated catalogue offered a 3½″ square lamp base in black. M'Kee offered the same item in an updated price list possibly of 1863, and in 1868 priced three sizes in black. These price lists, which have been reprinted, appear to be the earliest documentary proof that a specific factory in the United States was making black glass, other than bottle glass, at a specific date. Lamp bases were occasionally made in black through the rest of the century.

A novel type of art glass appeared in New England in 1878. Late in that year, the Mount Washington Glass Company introduced its Sicilian ware. This was glass made from a formula including volcanic lava, and in most pieces made is black. Into this were set irregular pieces of colored glass or lava. While some pieces with attractive color contrasts were produced, Sicilian ware evidently was not a sales success, as very little is found today. Illustrations may be seen in several books, including Revi's *Nineteenth Century Glass*.

As far as can be determined, there was before 1900 only one brief attempt by a manufacturer in the United States to market a set of black glass tableware. This occurred in 1891, when the Buckeye Glass Company, of Martins Ferry, Ohio, advertised in black a line which can be identified from trade journal descriptions. This is the pattern known as Fan Base or Windermere's Fan, which has not been attributed to Buckeye until now. That the attempt failed is attested by its rarity in black today. Examples may be seen in James' *Black Glass*.

About 1881-1883, various plates or plaques, some embossed with well-designed patterns, and other items were pressed of a dense opaque black glass by the West Side Glass Manufacturing Company, near Bridgeton, New Jersey. This glass, said to contain coal dust, was sold under the name Ferroline. Responsible for its introduction was an Italian in this country, one Enrico Rosenzi. In 1885 a new firm, the American Ferroline Comopany, took up its manufacture at New Brighton, Pennsylvania. Evidently neither firm had much commercial success with Rosenzi's formula, and production of Ferroline had ceased by the next year. Two pieces are pictured in *Spinning Wheel* for November, 1967.

Among other firms which made some black glass in the period 1881-1900 may be named Atterbury and Company, Dalzell, Gilmore and Leighton Company (Figure 342), Bonita Glass Company, and probably Model Flint Glass Company. None of these made much of the color.

Pieces from this period are not common today. Yet, it is interesting to note, Biser's 1899 *Elements of Glass and Glass Making* gives eleven different recipes for black, five of which were for flint glass. All eleven contained maganeses as a coloring agent. Manganese, used in smaller amounts, was the principal colorant in each of Biser's six recipes for purple glass, showing why much black glass can be seen by strong light to be purple.

Manganese, however, was merely a convenient ingredient of which to add enough to darken the glass to black. The purple or other color, not being visible in normal use, was of little or no concern to the manufacturer. Harry Bastow, a practical glassmaker, explained in 1908: "Black is commonly produced by using an excess of colorants which give effects that are largely complementary to each other, such as yellow, purple, blue, etc. This requires only that the colorants used should be compatible with the same batch conditions. The small amount of light that is transmitted through this glass is usually purple, blue, etc., according to which colorant is in the greatest excess, but this is rarely of sufficient importance to require careful balance for perfect neutralization, and as a matter of fact, black glass is commonly used as a dumping ground for using up cullet of any and all colors."

This, from an article entitled "Decorative Color Effects in Glass", implies that black glass items of more or less decorative appearance were being made in 1908, but where in this country is not known to me. One possibility is Pittsburg Lamp, Brass and Glass Company; see Figures 194 and 195.

In the fall of 1915, for possibly the first time in this country, an interest of American manufacturers in the wider use of black glass began to appear. On November 25 of that year, Westmoreland Specialty Company's New York display was described as including ornamental items in several colors, "newest of all, black". Cambridge Glass Company's black, it has been said, was new in late 1915; certainly it was on the market soon afterward. In January, 1916, Duncan and Miller displayed a few black items. In late March, Diamond Glass-Ware Company and H. Northwood Company were offering lines of black glass. Lancaster Glass Company and Fenton Art Glass Company also made black in 1916.

The trade journals, almost automatically, commented favorably on most of these lines, but any popularity they may have had seems to have been short-lived. Little black glass is found which can be attributed to these years. Fenton and Cambridge items are known, but are scarce. Most of those from other firms have not been identified. This is due in part to the fact that less has been published on glass of these years, other than carnival glass, than of some earlier and later periods. Also, some lines, especially those which were available with gold and enamel decorations, may have been of plain shapes, difficult to distinguish from those of later periods.

A Fenton catalogue of about 1921 picturing many such plain shapes in stretch glass (some pieces on unattached black bases) stated that they were also available in Ebony. The exact year of this catalogue may be questioned, but it is known that in 1922 two large firms, Cambridge and United States Glass Company, presented lines of occasional pieces in black. In 1923 New Martinsville Glass Manufacturing Company, Paden City Glass Manufacturing Company, Co-Operative Flint Glass Company, and others were working with black. In 1924 Fostoria Glass Company added its name to the list, but demand seems to have fallen off again about that time.

Black glass continued to be made in the next few years, but in a diminished role. United States Glass Company, possibly the leading exponent of black glass in the 1920's, continued to advertise it in many items

at least in 1925 and 1926, and in the latter year appeared the first indication of what was to be a continuing emphasis on black at Diamond Glass-Ware Company. Complete table settings of glass, including luncheon and dinner plates, were on the market in 1925, but were not then made in black. Some firms may have carried on little in black except the widely used bases on which to display bowls and vases, as in Figure 276.

The next resurgence of black, and the one which led to its greatest popularity, first becomes noticeable in 1929, with stemware leading the way. *The Pottery, Glass and Brass Salesman* observed on October 3: "One of the distinctive features of the year is medium and better grade glassware. It has been the range of suites black stemmed and black-footed ware topped by crystal bowls." "The novelty . . . of the combination" was also mentioned. The article went on to promote several such stemware lines from Morgantown Glass Works, which had just enlarged its selection of them, and implied that numerous other firms had been competing in this clear-and-black combination. However, the only others which can be named at present offering clear-and-black stemware in 1929 were Fostoria Glass Company and Central Glass Works. Fostoria's black-based line of that year had a square foot; so did one of Morgantown's styles, according to the article just quoted.

1929 saw also the first production in this century of table setting in black. It is not definitely known who was the first manufacturer, but Co-Operative Flint advertised "dinner sets in black glass" in that year. The trend to black gloomed in 1930; many companies were making it, and at least four — New Martinsville, Fostoria, Diamond, and Fenton — were making sets of black tableware. At the same time that the popularity of black spread out from the feet of drinking vessels, so did the square shape, coming to be boldly displayed in plates and everything that accompanied them. This trend can be seen in Figures 59, 60, 109, 123-125, and many others.

Black remained strong in 1931, possibly the all-time peak year of its popularity. By then, a large share of the demand for glassware for home use was being filled by automatic machinery. The relatively new machine-made colored glass tableware by Hocking, Jeannette Glass Company, Hazel-Atlas, and others was enjoying tremendous sales. Surprisingly, this was not true in black glass. Two black luncheon sets are credited to Hazel-Atlas, and some L. E. Smith vases appear to have been machine-blown, but most black glass items continued to be hand-pressed or hand-blown.

The present state of research allows only a vague sketch of the next few years. Apparently in 1932 sales of black took a sharp downturn; this was reflected in the small attention that manufacturers seem to have given black in designing new items for 1933. Handmade glass in colors in general also fell off steeply. The decline in production likely continued in 1934 and 1935.

There is little evidence available of black in the second half of the decade; however, Cambridge evidently continued Ebony until at least 1939, making vases and other pieces with gold decorations about that year. Fostoria still carried a few table items in Ebony in 1941. Some smaller companies must also have offered odd pieces.

During World War II, difficulties in obtaining ingredients curtailed seriously the manufacture of colored glass. In 1943 Imperial Glass Corporation was making Black Suede (Figure 505), but almost no black of the next several years has as yet been identified.

For 1949, Westmoreland Glass Company introduced black in a variety of items (Figures 312, 569), which it promoted vigorously in trade journal advertising. Its production lasted at least to the mid-1950's, by which time Cambridge, Fostoria, Viking, and others had entered the field.

In the last thirty years numerous glass companies have made some black on occasion. Possibly the most successful have been Westmoreland Glass Company (Figure 568 and others) and the Indiana Glass Division of Lancaster Colony Corporation (Figure 584 and following). Practically a new specialty appeared with the proliferation in the early 1980's of figurines and other small novelties, often in limited editions; many of these have been made in wide color ranges including black (Figures 623-657).

SOURCES: McKearin and Wilson, pp. 8-11, 100-103, 186 ff.; Biser, pp. 26, 27, 47, 93, 140, 141, 146; Munsey, pp. 37, 60, 116, 250; James Jackson Jarves, "Ancient and Modern Venetian Glass of Murano", *Harper's New Monthly Magazine*, vol. 64, December, 1881-May, 1882, pp. 177, 182, 188, 190; Corning et al, *Czechoslovakian Glass 1350-1980*, pp. 32, 33, 67, 150, 151; Newman, pp. 53, 155, 156, 351; Godden, *Illustrated Encyclopedia of British Pottery and Procelain*, pp. xix, 18, 31, 39, 164, etc.; Spillman, pp. 13-15, 87, 113, 358, 359, 388; McKearin, pp. 149, 186, 187, 267, 305, 314, 320, 340, 367, and pls. 107, 113; Lee, *Sandwich Glass*, pp. 47, 88-90, 132, 165, 268, 440-449, 495, 506, 530, 532, 533, and pls. 77, 207; Godden, *Antique Glass and China*, pp. 71-75; Lattimore, pp. 49, 55, 122-126; Manley, pp. 98, 99, 116, 117; Lagerberg 4, Figures 269, 274; Lee and Rose, pp. 51, 79, 80, 191, and pls. 6, 49; Rose, p. 108; Jarves, pp. 105-108; M'Kee and Brothers, pp. 40, 72, 113, 141; Thuro 2, pp. 24, 31-33, 49, 56, 57, 60, 68, 81, 85, 109; Smith, *Findlay Pattern Glass*, inside front cover and pp. 21, 27, 103; Measell and Smith, p. 98; Revi, *Nineteenth Century Glass*, pp. 231, 234, and plate facing p. 78; Albert Christian Revi, "Ferroline", *Spinning Wheel*, November, 1967, pp. 22, 24; Revi, *APGFB*, pp. 250, 251; Welker, *Pressed Glass in America*, p. 77; Grover, pp. 55, 58; Covill, pp. 278-280, 287, 288; Neal, p. 132; *P&GR*, February 27, 1890, and January 1, 1891; *CG&L*, January 14, 1891, January 10, 1916, p. 20, and June 12, 1916, p. 9; Lechner, pp. 86, 87; Heacock, *1000 Toothpick Holders*, pp. 35, 62; James, pp. 26, 27; Ferson, p. 127; *NGB*, January 20, 1900; "The Man Who Saw", *PG&BS*, November 25, 1915, p. 13, and October 3, 1929, p. 23; Phyllis Smith, "Cambridge Corner", *GR*, September, 1981, p. 40; "New Line at the Diamond", *CG&L*, March 27, 1916; "The Metropolitan Market", unidentified trade journal, March 30, 1916, p. 11; William Heacock, "Fenton's Ebony", *GR*, Winter, 1983, p. 12; *CCG*, pp. 8, 9; Harry Bastow, "Decorative Color Effects in Glass", *Glass and Pottery World*, April, 1908, as quoted in Thuro 2, p. 15; *F 1*, p. 88; "Among the Pittsburgh Displays", *CG&L*, January 23, 1922, p. 15; "New York Trade Notes", *CG&L*, March 27, 1922, p. 15; *W 2*, pp. 10, 11, 49, 51-53, 108, 109, 111, 149, 228, 231, 263, 269, 288, 301, 338-342; *WPT 2*, pp. 46, 258; *WFG*, pp. 109, 194, 195, 216; *F 2*, pp. 5, 18, 82; Mark Nye, "Cambridge Corner", *GR*, April, 1987, pp. 24, 25; Welker, *Co. 1*, p. 18; "Anne Visits Cambridge Glass Company", *CG&L*, September, 1942, as quoted in Mark Nye, "Cambridge Corner", *GR*, September, 1986, p. 8; "The Question-Box", *GR*, February, 1977, p. 45.

MAKERS OF BLACK GLASS

Following are the names of firms which have made black glass (other than bottles) in the United States, with the factory locations and dates at which black glass has been made.

This list has been compiled to be as inclusive as possible; however, in the present state of research, it cannot approach completeness, either in the number of factories or in the dates of manufacture. While most of the factories named have been established with reasonable certainty as makers of black glass, some which are questionable are marked with an asterisk.

It should be noted that some of these firms have operated also other factories than those with which this book is concerned.

Akro Agate Company, Clarksburg, West Virginia: about 1944-about 1947

Aladdin Industries, Incorporated, Alexandria, Indiana: 1936-1937

American Ferroline Company, New Brighton, Pennsylvania: 1885

Anchor Hocking Glass Corporation, location undetermined among several in various states: 1958?

Atterbury and Company, Pittsburgh, Pennsylvania: 1881

*Bellaire Goblet Company, Findlay, Ohio: (operated 1888-1891)

Big Pine Key Glass Works, Big Pine Key, Florida: date undetermined (in operation about 1972)

Bonita Glass Company, Cicero, Indiana: 1900

*Boston and Sandwich Glass Company, Sandwich, Massachusetts: 1850's?

Botson Mould and Glass, Norwich, Ohio: 1979-about 1984

Joseph Bournique and Company, Reading, Pennsylvania: 1884

Bernard Boyd, Cambridge, Ohio: dates undetermined (operated 1978-1983)

Boyd's Crystal Art Glass, Incorporated, Cambridge, Ohio: 1984

Bryce Brothers Company, Mount Pleasant, Pennsylvania: in the 1930's

Buckeye Glass Company, Martins Ferry, Ohio: 1890-1891

Cambridge Glass Company, Cambridge, Ohio: 1915-1916, 1924-1925, 1928, 1931, 1933-1934, 1937, 1939, 1950, 1954

Canton Glass Company, Marion, Indiana: 1896-1897

Canton Glass Company (the second firm of this name), Marion, Indiana: 1951

Central Glass Works, Wheeling, West Virginia: 1923-1924, 1929, about 1931

*Challinor, Taylor and Company, Tarentum, Pennsylvania (operated 1885-1891)

*Columbia Glass Company, Findlay, Ohio: 1888

Consolidated Lamp and Glass Company, Coraopolis, Pennsylvania: 1925

Co-Operative Flint Glass Company, Beaver Falls, Pennsylvania: 1923-1924, 1928-1929

Donna and Terry Crider, Wapakoneta, Ohio: 1982

Dalzell, Gilmore and Leighton Company, Findlay, Ohio: 1889?, 1897

Degenhart's Crystal Art Glass, Cambridge, Ohio: 1975 or earlier, 1976

Diamond Glass-Ware Company, Indiana, Pennsylvania: 1916, 1923, 1926-1931

*Dithridge and Company, Pittsburgh, Pennsylvania: 1899?

Duncan and Miller Glass Company, Washington, Pennsylvania: 1916, 1931, 1933

*Eagle Glass and Manufacturing Company, Wellsburg, West Virginia: 1899?

Economy Glass Company, Morgantown, West Virginia: 1926, 1929

Economy Tumbler Company, Morgantown, West Virginia: 1923

Fenton Art Glass Company, Williamstown, West Virginia: 1916, 1921?, 1922-1935, 1953-1954, 1962-1966, 1968-1976, 1981-1982

Fostoria Glass Company, Moundsville, West Virginia: 1924-1941, 1953-1957, 1982

H. C. Fry Glass Company, Rochester, Pennsylvania: 1929-1930

Gibson Glass, Milton, West Virginia: 1984

*C. Granger and Company, Vernon, New York: (operated 1833-before 1842)

*C. and O. Granger, Vernon, New York: (operated before 1842-1844)

*Charles Granger and Company, Vernon, New York: (operated 1824?-1829?)

Granger, James and Company?, Mount Pleasant, New York: date undetermined (operated 1844?-1850's?)

*Granger, Southworth and Company, Vernon, New York: (operated 1829?-1833)

Hazel-Atlas Glass Company, location(s) undetermined among several in various states: early 1930's?

*Hemingray Glass Company, Covington, Kentucky: 1879?

L. J. Houze Convex Glass Company, Point Marion, Pennsylvania: 1931 or later

Huntington Tumbler Company, Huntington, West Virginia: 1930-1931

Imperial Glass Company, Bellaire, Ohio: about late 1920's and 1931

Imperial Glass Corporation, Bellaire, Ohio: 1932, 1943, 1954-1955, about 1966, 1979, 1981-1983

Indiana Glass Company, Dunkirk, Indiana: 1973-1978, 1980-1987

Lancaster Glass Company, Lancaster, Ohio: 1931-1933?

*Libbey Glass Company, Toledo, Ohio: about 1910?-about 1920?

Libbey Glass Manufacturing Company, Toledo, Ohio: 1933

Liberty Works, Egg Harbor, New Jersey: 1930, 1931?

Louie Glass Company, Weston, West Virginia: 1930

McKee Glass Company, Jeannette, Pennsylvania: 1922?, 1923, 1930-1931, 1932?

M'Kee and Brothers, Pittsburgh, Pennsylvania: 1864,1868

Model Flint Glass Company, Findlay, Ohio: date undetermined (operated 1888-1893)

Morgantown Glassware Guild, Morgantown, West Virginia: 1965?

Morgantown Glass Works, Morgantown, West Virginia: 1929-1932, 1934

Mosser Glass, Incorporated, Cambridge, Ohio: 1983. (Thick items in amethyst and smoke colors, which have been made at least since 1981, also may appear black.)

*Mount Vernon Glass Company, Vernon, New York: (operated 1810 or 1811-about 1824)

Mount Washington Glass Company, New Bedford, Massachusetts: about 1878

*National Glass Company, Marion, Indiana: (operated 1899-1902)

New Martinsville Glass Manufacturing Company, New Martinsville, West Virginia: 1923, 1926?, 1931-1932, 1935

H. Northwood Company, Wheeling, West Virginia: 1916, about 1925

John Nygren, Walnut Cove, North Carolina: 1980

Paden City Glass Manufacturing Company, Paden City, West Virginia: 1923, 1931, 1933, 1936

Pairpoint Corporation, New Bedford, Massachusetts: about 1920

*Justus Perry, Kenne, New Hampshire: (operated 1817-1822)

Pilgrim Glass Corporation, Ceredo, West Virginia: 1984

*Pittsburg Lamp, Brass and Glass Company,

location undetermined (among several in Pennsylvania): 1906 or 1907?

Pittsburgh Plate Glass Company, location undetermined (among several in various states): 1923

Plum Glass Company, Pittsburgh, Pennsylvania: 1987

Seneca Glass Company, Morgantown, West Virginia: 1931, 1976, 1981

H. P. Sinclaire and Company, Bath, New York: 1920-not later than 1923

L. E. Smith Glass Company, Greensburg Glass Works, Greensburg, Pennsylvania: late 1920's?-early 1930's?

L. E. Smith Glass Company, Mount Pleasant, Pennsylvania: mid 1920's?-about 1935, 1950's?

*Sneath Glass Company, Hartford City, Indiana: 1936?

Steuben Glass Works, Corning, New York: about 1917?, 1926-1932

Thames Street Glass House, Newport, Rhode Island: 1982 or 1983

Tiffin Glass Company, Tiffin, Ohio: early 1970's?

*United States Glass Company, Findlay, Ohio, Factory M (operated 1891-1892)

*United States Glass Company, Gas City, Indiana: late 1920's-early 1930's?

*United States Glass Company, Glassport, Pennsylvania: late 1920's?-early 1930's?

*United States Glass Company, Pittsburgh, Pennsylvania (factory(ies) undetermined several in Pittsburgh): late 1920's?-early 1930's

United States Glass Company, Tiffin, Ohio: 1922-1935, 1949?-1952?

Viking Glass Company, New Martinsville, West Virginia: 1950, 1981

*Vineland Flint Glass Works, Vineland, New Jersey: about 1931?

Westmoreland Glass Company, Grapeville, Pennsylvania: 1923?, 1929?, 1930-1931, early 1940's? 1949, 1951-1952, 1953?, 1954-1955, 1967, about 1971, 1981

Westmoreland Specialty Company, Grapeville, Pennsylvania: 1915

West Side Glass Manufacturing Company, Bridgeton, New Jersey: about 1883

R. Wetzel Glass Company, Zanesville, Ohio: 1975, 1981

DESCRIPTION OF COLOR PAGES

Front Cover

Figure 1 (upper left): "A particularly outstanding number is the 'Rebecca' vase", noted *The Pottery, Glass and Brass Salesman*, reviewing McKee Glass Company's wares on February 9, 1928. This vase was made, in a variety of transparent and opaque colors, until around 1934. Height, 12". References: Stout, *McKee*, pp. 97, 103, 107; *W 2*, p. 267; "The History of the McKee Glass Company", 1929 article, reprinted in *Daze*, February, 1979, p. 8.

Figure 2 (upper right): The bowl or basin appears to be in Cambridge Glass Company's Community pattern, which was made in Ebony between about 1915 and 1923. A Cambridge catalogue shows this basin with a straight-sided pitcher, paneled to near the top. The identity of the pitcher shown here is unknown. References: Welker, *Co.* 1, p. 107, and 2, p. 5; Bennett, p. 35; *CCG*, pp. 8, 9, 12, 13, 16-19; Mark Nye, "Cambridge Corner", *GR*, December, 1985, p. 15.

Figure 3 (lower left): This tulip design plate was item 31 in Cambridge's Everglade pattern. Introduced in 1933, this item was offered until at least 1936, and reappeared in milk-white briefly in 1954. Everglade was advertised in several colors in the 1930's, but is seldom seen in Ebony. References: *CGC 1*, pl. 33-29B and p. 34-19; *W 2*, p. 42; Welker, *Co.* 1, p. 70; *CGC 2*, p. W5; Welker, *Color 2*, pl. 6.

Figure 4 (lower right) shows the larger of two sizes of elephant covered dish brought out by Co-Operative Flint Glass Company about 1927. In this size, about 13" long, it is rare today. This example has a satin finish, a feature seldom associated with Co-Operative's glass. The smaller size, about 7" long and 4½" high, has been remade in clear and colors in the 1980's, probably by Indiana Glass, and sold by Tiara Exclusives. Other manufacturers of these dishes have also been reported; however, the situation is complicated by another very similar dish, with the elephant's trunk higher. It is of uncertain origin, and may not exist in black. References: *W 2*, p. 50; *WPT 2*, pp. 11, 58; Van Pelt, p. 14; Mary Van Pelt, "Fantastic Figurines", *Best of GR 3*, pp. 76, 77; Stout, *DG 2*, pl. 10; Ferson, pp. 106, 107; "What's New?", *GR*, November, 1984, p. 16; "Tiara Exclusives", *Daze*, May 1, 1985, p. 30, May 1, 1986, p. 41, and May 1, 1987, p. 41; Millard, *Opaque Glass*, pl. 315.

Figures 5-14: **Cambridge Glass Company,** except as noted.

5. Set made up of #214 handled tray, circa 1930-1931, holding #1070 pinch decanter and clear stopper, circa 1928-1933, and four clear #1070 2 oz. pinch tumblers, circa 1928-1949. The mold for this decanter was revised to add pointed ornaments on the sides, with which it appears in catalogues of 1934 and later. At least three styles of stopper were used.

6. Tally-Ho pattern #1402/52 ice pail, introduced 1932, in chromium plated frame from Farber Brothers; height excluding handle, 5½". The combination shown was available, at least in transparent colors, in 1935.

7. #1 keg set, circa 1926-1930, in Ebony and light Emerald. Diameter of tray, 10".

8. #3400/119 ball shaped 12 oz. cordial decanter with clear handle and stopper, circa 1933-1949, in Farber Brothers marked metal holder.

9. Statuesque pattern #3011/9 3 oz. cocktail, introduced circa 1931 and made as late as 1956 at the Cambridge factory. Those made in the earlier years have optic ribbing in the bowl; later ones, made probably after about 1940, do not. The cocktail with the Ebony stem and clear bowl and foot is pictured on a catalogue page from 1949 or 1950. It is reported that Imperial Glass Corporation also made it in this combination, using former Cambridge molds, in the 1960's.

10. #1327 1 oz. cordial or #0379 vase (probably the same item), circa 1933-1941.

11A, B, C. Maker unknown. These three decanters could be mistaken for the Cambridge #1070 shown in Figure 5. Notice the much wider neck on the Figure 11 bottles, as well as the difference in body shape. These silver deposit designs are not among those offered by Cambridge in 1931.

12A-D. "Game Set", four 10 oz. footed tumblers, clear with Heart and Diamond feet in Carmen, Club and Spade Feet in Ebony; introduced in 1949 or 1950.

13. Maker unknown. This appears to differ slightly from plain ice buckets identified as made by Fenton, Fostoria, and others.

14. Decagon #851 ice bucket, circa 1928-1940.

15. Maker uncertain, probably in the 1930's. This quart-size cocktail shaker appears identical in shape with ones made by Duncan and Miller, Hazel-Atlas, and New Martinsville; Hazel-Atlas may have used a metal top like the one shown. The silver deposit, marked Sterling, resembles but does not match Cambridge's Imperial Hunt etching.

16. Possibly Cambridge Glass Company's #1917/232 lemon tub of the early 1920's, with unidentified silver deposit decoration; size 5".

17. Maker unknown, paneled comport or bowl on foot, flared, height 6", diameter 8¾", likely made between 1915 and 1930.

18 and 19. Two of Cambridge Glass Company's famous swans, which were made in many colors, from 1928 to the mid-1950's. Seven sizes were made, from 3" to 16" according to catalogue measurements, which did not include the upper neck and head. Over the years some changes were made in feather detail and wing position.

Figure 18 shows the 3" size (#1040) in the style made from 1933 to about 1950. This size with no fine details in the feathers, as made by Cambridge in the 1950's, has been reproduced by Mosser Glass, Inc. from 1975 or earlier to the present.

Figure 19 shows the 10" size (#1044) in the style offered in 1930, which was replaced by 1949 with a version lacking details in the feathers.

20. Possibly a Diamond Glass-Ware Company product advertised in 1925, this comport stood on a serving plate to make a cheese and cracker set. The example here is 4½" across, 3" high, and has a silver-decorated rim.

21. Cambridge #627 candlestick, circa 1927-1936, sometimes catalogued as part of Centennial or other tableware lines.

22. Maker unknown, 5¼" cupped bowl with distinctive feet, possibly 1920's.

23. Cambridge #1341 1 oz. cordial, 1933-1937.

24. Cambridge Decagon #865 cup, circa 1928-1931.

25. Fostoria #2350 Pioneer after dinner cup and saucer, in black circa 1929-1941.

26. Cambridge #973 5½" square tray with two handles, circa 1928-1932, used to hold four tumblers or creamer, sugar, salt and pepper.

27. Maker unknown, 3½" square box, possibly 1930's.

28. Cambridge #880 tray of bridge set (tray and four tumblers), clubs, hearts, diamonds and spades are molded into tray, circa 1928-1931.

29. Possibly Cambridge Glass Company's #3000 footed tumbler, 3 oz., circa 1927-1937, and #693 plate, circa 1929-1937 (together, #693/3000 canape set), with silver bands and monogram.

30. Cambridge #118 basket, listed in catalogues as 8" (width of opening), circa 1922-1929. The matching #119 7" was offered as late as around 1937.

31. Maker unknown, 9" vase.

32. Fostoria's #2360 vase, circa 1926-1931, in 10" size, also made in 8" size.

33. Maker uncertain, basket, likely made between 1915 and 1925. A vase in a similar design, #2586, appeared in Cambridge catalogues circa 1910-1915.

34. Cambridge ball shaped 80 oz. jug, matching the 3400 line of tableware. This jug was made 1931-1949, sometimes with various optic designs, and was variously designated as #3400/38, #3143/38, and Corinth #3900/116.

35. Cambridge 8½" footed bowl with ram's head handles, pattern number uncertain, circa 1925-1926, rare in black. A 1927 catalogue shows this bowl with small ornaments on each side midway between the ram's heads, ribs on top of the foot, and other changes in details, as #432. A further revised version, with a scalloped rim matching Cambridge's Gadroon pattern, was introduced in 1933 as #3500/25.

36. Cambridge #935 64 oz. jug, made 1927-circa 1931 with the angular handle shown here, and later in the 1930's with a curved handle. Each type was also made with an ice lip, as #956. The piece shown has an acid-etched monogram.

37A, B. Probably Westmoreland Glass Company's #1207 sugar and creamer, mid-1920's, with unidentified silver deposit decoration.

38. Maker unknown, Black Mantle* pint pitcher, possibly 1920's; no matching items are known.

39. Cambridge tray, pattern number unknown, 1930-circa 1937, used for salt and pepper shakers, or with a pair of #3400/96 2 oz. oils as an oil and vinegar set.

40. Cambridge tray of Decagon #1095 sugar and cream set, circa 1928-1932.

41. 6½" comport, probably made by Co-Operative Flint Glass Company, which advertised a candlestick of matching design in 1924. A similar design was made by United States Glass Company.

42. Cambridge Pristine #499 Calla Lily candlestick, hgt. 6", 1949-1950.

43. Cambridge Corinth #3900/575 cornucopia vase, mid-1949-1950, catalogued as 10", very similar to the Pristine 575 9" made earlier.

44. Cambridge #94 sweet pea vase, hgt. 7", diameter 8½", circa 1922-1927.

45. Cambridge #647 candelabra, sometimes treated as part of the #3400 line. Note the pair of small projections at top center and the ten-sided foot of the example shown, which was made probably in 1930. By 1931, a taller finial had been added in the center; between 1934 and 1938 the ten-sided foot became round, and was made so at least until 1952. One- and three-light candleholders of the same basic design were also made.

46. Fostoria Glass Company's #2538 place card holder with nut dish or ash tray, hgt. 2½", introduced about 1936, catalogued in Ebony after 1950.

47. Cambridge Decagon #984 bowl, 10" per catalogues, 12½" including handles, circa 1928-1932.

48. Viking Glass Company's #951/1S oval celery with clear swan handle, said to date between 1940 and 1960.

49. Unidentified 5" flower holder (?)

50. Cambridge #3400/90 2 compartment relish, about 6", 7¾" including handles, 1931-1949.

51. Viking Glass Company's #1007 1-light "Flowerlite", cupped bowl with a clear flower frog with a candle hole in the center, catalogued as 4½" (approximate height), possibly in the 1950's.

52. Westmoreland Glass Company's 5" spade-shaped ash tray of #1820 Ace 4-piece card set. The set of ash trays shaped to represent the card suits was made in the 1920's, colors unknown, and about 1971, when it was offered in "Assorted Colors", the spade being shown in black.

53. Cambridge Pristine #493 square candlestick, 2¾" per catalogues, made 1940-1954, listed in 1952 as Cambridge Square #3797/493; offered in Ebony around 1950; also made in 1¾" and 3¾" sizes.

55. Maker unknown, footed bowl, six-scallop rim, gilt on edge; made about the late 1920's-mid 1930's, when Fostoria made a very similar bowl.

56. Maker unknown, 12 oz. footed tumbler, clear bowl on black foot domed in the center, possibly 1929-1935.

57. Maker unknown, 12¾" six-scallop bowl of the same period as Figure 55.

58. Maker unknown, 7″ candlestick with molded all-over design imitating crackled glass. Various factories made lines on this order around 1926-early 1930's.

59, 60. Diamond Glass-Ware Company's #99 Charade* luncheon plate, cup and saucer. Black was the featured color in 1930 advertisements of this pattern, although it is known in dark blue, green, amethyst, and pink also. The plates, bowls, and saucers closely resemble Fenton's #1639 Jay Cee* pattern.

61. Maker unknown, pair of Ellen* candlesticks, one of which is turned to show the pattern on the underside of the foot, similar to that in Figure 58.

62. Woodpecker* wall vase, 8¼″ long, also called Hummingbird*. Fragments of this vase have been found at the site of the Diamond Glass-Ware Company, which probably made it in black at some time in the period 1926-1931. It is also known in transparent colors and in carnival glass.

63. Mary Ann* 2-handled vase, hgt. 6″, also called Cordelia*, well known in carnival glass. This vase is found with ten scallops in the top rim (as shown), and with only eight scallops. Other details differ between the two types. The eight-scallop type was made by Diamond Glass-Ware Company, around 1916 in opalescent; the maker and date of the ten-scallop one here are uncertain.

64. This 5″ Beaded Basket* is another novelty item better known in carnival glass. While shards have been found at the Diamond Glass-Ware Company site, the date of production is uncertain—in black, probably circa 1916 or 1926-1931. Other pattern names are Basketweave (B), seldom used, and Big Basketweave, which belongs to another pattern.

65. Diamond Glass-Ware Company's 7¾″ vase, number uncertain, also made with top flared (#5122), circa 1930. This design matches Diamond's Barcelona line of tableware and other items, introduced in 1928. The example here has silver deposit decoration. The mold for this vase was evidently acquired by Fenton Art Glass Company, which used it with distinctive colors, mostly cased and opalescent, around 1939.

66. Greensburg Glass Works' #1018 6″ vase, about 1925-1935.

67. 3″ flower pot, probably by L. E. Smith Glass Company, which made others apparently related, circa 1930.

68. L. E. Smith #1000 fan vase, circa mid-1920's-mid-1930's, also made flared and cupped (Figure 261). Note the 8-sided foot. Fenton made similar vases, but having a round foot, in many colors, circa 1926-1938.

69. Black flowers in two sizes, maker unknown, possibly of the same era as the vase holding them. Both stems and heads are of glass, the blooms are coated with silver. Lengths, 7½″ and 13½″. Rare.

70A, B. Greensburg's handled sugar bowl #5029-2, lacking cover, and #5029 handled creamer, about 1925-1930.

71. 2″ figure of walking horse, marked with C in circle (copyright), reportedly made by L. E. Smith, also in clear glass (1920's?) and in late years in frosted clear.

72. L. E. Smith horse bookend, made in black probably in the 1950's, in frosted clear as late as 1982. Very similar horse bookends were made by Fostoria, and reportedly by New Martinsville and Viking Glass Companies.

73. Rearing horse figurine, 2½″ tall, marked with C in circle, reportedly made by L. E. Smith circa 1930's and, in frosted clear, in recent years.

74. 7″ swan dish, silver decorated, marked with C in circle. This design, probably in 9″ size, is #3/4 (in black) and #3/10 (milk-white) in L. E. Smith literature of about 1930. This has seldom been called Kimberly*, a name of other patterns.

75. Kitten Paperweight*, 1¼″ high, marked C in circle, probably made by L. E. Smith in the 1920's or 1930's. A larger cat which may match this was #6642, shown in frosted clear in Smith's 1980 catalogue. Rare in carnival glass.

76A, B, C. Three Scotty Dogs, all made by L. E. Smith, possibly in the 1930's. A and B seem to be the #6652 3″ and #6653 5″ offered in frosted clear in Smith's 1980 catalogue, and 1½″ C seems to belong to the same family.

77. Dog ash tray, 4″ across, also made in 6¼″ size by Greensburg Glass Works, about late 1920's-mid-1930's.

78. Greensburg's #2 elephant ash tray, about 6″ diameter, also made in 4″ size, in the same period as above.

79. Greensburg's #1 dog cigarette box and cover, 2½″ x 3½″, matching Figure 77; also made with elephant on lid (#2), matching Figure 78.

80. Maker uncertain. Possibly Greensburg's #81-3 mayonnaise ladle, but other factories made very similar ladles in the 1920's.

81. L. E. Smith's #635 footed square mayonnaise bowl, silver decorated, probably early 1930's.

82. Greensburg's #681 celery dish, about 1930.

Figures 83-94: **Fenton Art Glass Company,** except as noted.

83. Double Dolphin* #1533 fan vase, circa 1927-1929, also called Twin Dolphins*. This shape was reintroduced in black in 1980 as #7551, marked Fenton. See also Figure 102.

84. Large oval bowl, circa 1928. This bowl and a smaller matching one, Fenton's #1621, were shaped in various ways while hot.

85. Five-legged base, used with bowls and vases of various colors, circa 1932-1935.

86A, B. Possibly Fenton's #1611 Agua Caliente or Georgian line tumblers, 5″ and 4″, circa 1930-1935. Many factories have made tumblers of this pattern.

87. Maker unknown, 10¼″ shallow cupped bowl, circa 1920-1925.

88. Six-Ring* sugar bowl, circa 1930.

89. Possibly Fenton's #607 shallow bowl, circa 1921; 9¼″ diameter.

90. Fenton's #1502 Diamond Optic tray of dresser set, circa 1927; 8″ long.

91. Flower stopper, 2¼″, possibly #55½, circa 1925. This design was also used as the handle on the lid of Fenton's #844 candy box, circa 1927-1938.

92. Maker uncertain, bath salts jar, 4½″ tall, apparently advertised in milk white about 1942. Fenton made a similar or the same jar with a different stopper about 1929.

93. Basket, probably Fenton Art Glass Company's Basketweave Base*, reportedly #1092, possibly circa 1916. Fenton's #8222 Basket Weave bowl, made in many colors since 1970, marked with the name Fenton, is virtually identical, but some similar items in earlier catalogues have only 16 pairs of openings in the border, whereas this has 18. See also Figure 463.

94. Fenton Basketweave Base candleholder, about 1930-1936, 5″ diameter.

Figures 95-108: **Fenton Art Glass Company,** except as noted.

95. #919 high footed orange bowl, circa 1916, rare in black. The exterior pattern is Fenton's Cherry*; the pattern inside the bowl (not visible here) is Mikado* (it should be specified as Fenton's, since there are other patterns named Mikado). Another name for this piece is Cherries and Mums*.

96. Flared console bowl with flower block and Nymph figure (Fenton reportedly called this September Morn Nymph), circa 1928-1936, all #1234. The figure may have been numbered 1645 and 1522 also.

97. Probably Fenton's original #1234 candleholder, circa 1929-1932; a somewhat different style carried this number in the next few years. Diameter 4″.

98. Persian Medallions* high footed bowl, 7″, possibly made in 1916. Fenton made this pattern circa 1911-1917, and again from 1970. In the latter years this piece, with the top variously shaped, has been numbered 8234, 9422, and 9623.

99. #184 vase, about 12″ tall, with a Fenton cutting, circa 1931-1934. Fenton made this in 6″, 8″, 10″ and 12″ sizes. Vases of nearly identical shape were made by Cambridge (#402, #782), Imperial (#775, #7751), Paden City (also #184), and possibly others.

100, 101. #6 Swan candlestick and oval bowl, date of production in black uncertain. These pieces were hand-worked into somewhat different shapes in frosted clear about 1938; the candlestick, with alterations, was made in carnival glass in the 1970's. Also called Swan Lake*.

102. Double Dolphin* #1623 candlestick, circa 1927-1937. This may be found in various colors, with ribbing or an embossed floral design on the underside of the foot. Another name is Swirled Dolphin*.

103. #1565 Turtle flower bowl, circa 1927-1929, also offered with a lid as a bon-bon, or as a base to hold the #1538 blown aquarium.

104. #1639 Jay Cee* jug, circa 1930-1933.

105. 5″ vase, pattern unidentified, probably made by Imperial Glass Corporation, which made similar four-footed vases in other patterns, with the same open-work rim design, from the 1930's to the 1960's.

106. 3½″ shaving mug, W · 111 when in Moonstone color (black may have been designated by a different number), circa 1933.

107. Rose Spray* #2 mug, 3½″, 9 oz., circa 1916. This is sometimes called simply the Rose Mug or Fenton Rose Mug, but this could be confusing as Rose is the name of a Fenton color. Shown in old ads as 42¢ a dozen.

108. #107 tulip vase, circa 1932-1933.

Figures 109-118: **Fostoria Glass Company,** except as noted.

109. Pair of #2453 lustres, each with eight prisms; probably of the mid-1950's, though the shape was made as early as 1932.

110. Maker unknown, 11″ rolled edge bowl, about 1920-early 1930's.

111. Fostoria's Lotus #318 low candlestick, clear bowl with Ebony base, introduced January, 1982. See also Figure 121.

112. Westmoreland Glass Company's #1921 4½″ compote, circa 1971. The #1921 pattern was called Lotus in the 1920's, but this shape may not have been made at that time. See also Figures 316, 572, and 575.

113. #2638 Contour candlestick, 4½ x 5″, circa 1954-1957.

114. #2297 deep bowl "A", circa 1928-early 1930's.

115. #2324 3″ candlestick (catalogued by Fostoria as 4″), probably circa 1927-1934. This shape was later numbered 2324/315, and by 1982 simply 314.

116. Probably Fostoria's #2350 Pioneer dinner plate, 9½″ diameter (Fostoria listed 9″ and 10″ sizes), circa 1929-1941.

117. #2375 Fairfax lemon dish, 7″ plus handles, circa 1930-1942.

118. #2375 Fairfax cracker plate, circa 1930-1942, with unidentified silver decoration. Apparently the same shape was called a cake plate when made without the indentation in the center, seen here, to seat a footed cheese plate.

Figures 119-130: **Fostoria Glass Company.**

119. #2428 13″ vase, made in Ebony in the period circa 1927-1934 and in the mid-1950's; also made in 6″ and 9″ sizes.

120. #2288 Tut vase, probably mid-1950's.

121. Lotus #323 high candlestick, clear bowl with Ebony base, 7¾″ tall. See also Figure 111. Fostoria's Lotus pattern, introduced in January, 1982, included also five stemmed drinking vessels and a bud vase, each available with clear bowl and Crystal Mist, Ebony, or Peach Mist base.

122. #2395½ candlestick, made in black circa 1928-1929 and probably for several years following.

123. #2419 Mayfair 4-part relish, shape made circa 1930-1936, in black in at least 1931.

124. #2419 Mayfair dinner plate, shape made circa 1930-1934, in black in at least 1931.

125. #2350½ Pioneer footed cup, probably of the 1929-1941 period, and #2419 Mayfair saucer, both offered in black in at least 1931. Fostoria frequently combined these cup and saucer shapes.

126A, B. #2350½ Pioneer footed sugar and footed cream, probably of the period 1929-1941, definitely offered in Ebony in 1931.

127. #2320 nappy cupped "B", circa 1925.

128. #1681 wall vase, about 1927-1928. The same item made slightly earlier was flat rather than curved across the top of the back.

129. #2402 bowl, made in Ebony about 1929 and again in the mid-1950's.

130. #2402 candlestick, mid-1950's.

131A, B. Hazel-Atlas Glass Company's Ovide* creamer and sugar, with Floral Sterling* silver deposit decoration (very worn), also attributed to Hazel-Atlas in the early 1930's. Another name is Mound Bayou*. These shapes are also known as New Century*, which was probably this company's name for another pattern. Figures 140-142 show the decoration more plainly.

132. 6″ vase, presumably Hazel-Atlas with Floral Sterling decoration. Hazel-Atlas, Florentine pattern vase is the same shape and size as this one.

133. Hazel-Atlas Cloverleaf creamer, early or mid-1930's.

134. Two Hazel-Atlas salt shakers decorated Floral Sterling. See Figures 131A and B.

135A, B, C. Three of Lancaster Glass Company's #533 shakers, 4¾″ high, with two styles of silver decoration, circa 1932. Hocking Glass Company carried on this shape later in the 1930's, but probably not in black glass.

136. Clear glass jar, circa 1920-1964, marked on the bottom with the Hazel-Atlas HA trademark and the number 5935-2, with black glass lid, perhaps not original, maker unknown, probably 1915-1935, and clear spoon, possibly made in the 1970's or 1980's by West Virginia Glass Specialty Company, Weston, West Virginia.

137. Hocking Glass Company's Block Optic #933 sherbet, green glass with black enamel fired on stem and foot, probably 1930. Hocking is said to have called this tableware pattern both Block Optic and Optic Block; today the name is often abbreviated to Block*.

138. Sugar server, possibly by Duncan and Miller Glass Company in the 1930's, with red plastic top, height 6″.

139. Possibly Hazel-Atlas #1533 salt and pepper shakers, with red plastic tops, 1930's; height 3″.

140-142. Ovide pieces with Floral Sterling decoration: (140) cup and saucer, (141) salad plate, (142) sherbet and sherbet plate. See Figures 131A and B, 132, 134.

143. Bowl, maker unknown, probably early 1930's, in design similar to Hazel-Atlas' Ribbon* pattern.

144. Cambridge Glass Company's #393 10″ 5-compartment relish, circa 1934.

145. Three-compartment candy or relish dish, maker uncertain, in ornate metal frame, possibly 1925-1935.

146. Imperial Glass Corporation's Candlewick #14200 (earlier #3400) goblet, made in black experimentally in the 1970's.

147. Imperial's #108 (later #51751) 6″ Rose vase with IG mark on bottom, black with satin finish, probably Black Suede of the 1950's.

148. Crimped bowl, maker uncertain, circa 1935, said to be from Imperial. Viking Glass Company later made a similar bowl, its #707.

149. Bowl with open work rim, 3½″ high, possibly made by L. E. Smith Glass Company circa 1953. Milk-white pieces in this pattern were advertised by a decorating firm in 1953 and by a wholesaler in 1972, in the latter year along with known Smith glass. A matching item is shown in Figure 305.

150, 152, 153A and B. Pieces of Imperial Glass Company's, and its successor Imperial Glass Corporation's, #682 Pillar Flute pattern, circa 1928-1937: (150) two-handled pickle, (152) 6½″ comport with flat rim, and (153A, B) sugar and cream set. This has also been pictured under the name Lustre and Clear*, apparently by mistaking it for the pattern by that name.

151. Imperial Glass Company's #330 Heavy Diamond* honey dish, square, 1928-1931. Other pattern names: Diamond Block*, Little Jewel*, New Jewel*.

154. 4″ nappy, possibly made by Liberty Works in 1930. Also appearing to match this are Imperial's Hazen*, made about 1937 and probably several years earlier, and a few items made by Morgantown in 1932.

155. Sauce boat, length 5¾″, unidentified pattern of wide panels, possibly made by Diamond Glass-Ware Company between 1926 and 1931, as this piece is very similar to the sauce boat in that firm's Victory pattern.

156, 157. Imperial Glass Company's Diamond Quilted* sherbet, 6 ounce size, with three-ring stem, and candle holder, 2½″ high (diamond pattern on underside of foot), about late 1920's. Other name: Flat Diamond*.

158. Imperial Glass Company's #7387 Alternating Flute and Panel* 7½″ bowl, circa 1930-1931.

159. 3″ candlestick with crimped foot, maker unknown, about 1925-1935.

160. Imperial Glass Corporation's #778 dolphin comporte (Imperial's spelling), 7¼″, in frosted black (Black Suede), about 1943-1955.

161. Imperial's Scottie Dog bookend, height 6½″. This example, in frosted black dated 1979, was made for the National Cambridge Collectors, Inc. The mold was formerly used by Cambridge Glass Company for its #1128 Scotty Dog bookend, which was made in black, probably in the late 1930's or early 1940's.

162. Pair of Imperial's Mandarin bookends, 7½″, made in black, it is reported, in only a small quantity in 1982. This design was earlier sold (not in black) as the Lu-Tung book holders, part of Imperial's Cathay line, said to represent an Immortal of Taoist religion.

163. 7″ vase, frosted, a piece of Imperial's Black Suede of about 1943-1955.

164 and 165. Two Hobnail* powder boxes, maker unknown, probably 1930-1935: (164) diameter 6½″, lacking cover, and (165) diameter 4½″, with cover. The Figure 165 box is also found with a different glass lid.

166. Maker unknown, Elegant* 4½″ swan-shaped dish, probably 1915-1940. This differs in only small details from Fenton's #4 Swan, made about 1937, and Imperial's #147 Swan, made about the same time and later. Dugan also made a similar swan, of which the exact details are unknown as yet, around 1906-1909, and H. Northwood Company is said to have been another maker. (It is not certain that all of the varieties were made in black.) It is unlikely that any of these swans were intended to be used as salt dishes, which they have sometimes been called. Some were made in pastel iridescent glass, hence the name Pastel Swan* has been given to one variety, possibly the one shown here. The name Little Swan* has also been used for this group, but belongs to a different item.

167. Imperial's Scolding Bird, reportedly made in black briefly in 1982 only. This example is marked with the name of its designer, Virginia B. Evans. Introduced in 1949 as Scolding Bird, part of Imperial's Cathay line, this figure was called #10 Nosy Jaybird in the 1960's, but the original name was reinstated by 1981.

168. Imperial's Phoenix bowl, 8″ long, 6″ high, in Black Suede, circa 1954-1955. This is another design based on mythology and first sold in the Cathay line.

169. Two-handled bowl, frosted, with painted floral decoration, maker uncertain, very similar to Imperial's #7257 Molly* two-handled bowl of about 1937. See also Figures 171, 172, 431, and 491.

170. Imperial Glass Company's Diamond Quilted* crimped nappy, frosted and painted with flowers, probably late 1920's or early 1930's. See also Figures 156 and 157.

171. Octagon saucer, possibly Morgantown Glass Works', 1932, or Imperial Glass Company's (or Corporation's) Molly pattern, 1930-circa 1937.

172. Salad plate, possibly Morgantown's #1517, made in 1932, or Imperial's Molly #7285D, 1930-circa 1937.

173. Paden City Glass Manufacturing Company's #412 Bee's Knees* or Crow's Foot Square* handled sandwich tray, 10″, etched with the Delilah Bird* design, reportedly by the same company, about 1929-1935. This etching has also been called Peacock Reverse*.

174. 9″ candlestick, maker uncertain. United States Glass Company's #76 candlestick, made 1927-circa 1929, and Paden City's #117, probably of the mid-1920's, are nearly identical in shape with this one, but about 8¼″ in height.

175. Paden City batter set, consisting of #11 batter jug and #11 syrup jug in clear with black covers and tray, 1936.

176. Mushroom-shaped 8″ jar, black with white cover, made by Morgantown Glassware Guild. The example

shown was bought at the Fostoria Glass Company factory after Fostoria acquired the Morgantown firm in 1965.

177. Morgantown Eggcentric candy jar, 5″, also made in other sizes, and with black lid on white base, probably 1950-1965. This example was bought at the factory.

178 and 179. Maker unknown, 12 ounce footed tumbler and matching seafood cocktail, clear with black foot, gold lines on edges of foot and bowl, date uncertain, possibly 1940-1960.

180. Maker unknown, sherbet, clear bowl with black stem and foot, most likely early 1930's.

181-183. L. E. Smith Glass Company's #3 cookie jar, 8″, (182) #1 cookie jar, 6¾″, and (183) #4 cookie jar, 5¾″, with painted morning glory, possibly applied by Smith; about 1927-1935.

184. McKee Glass Company's #157 Scallop Edge comport, probably early 1930's, decorated with flowers in rust and yellow. See also Figure 450.

185. Maker uncertain, vase, 8¾″ high, 9″ in diameter, similar to McKee's smaller #1004 globe vase which was made in the 1930's and probably earlier.

186. McKee's #25 jardiniere, 1931.

187. McKee's vase or jar (reportedly candy jar) and cover, probably early 1930's, offered without lid as #200 Art Nude; shown here decorated with gilt.

188. Maker unknown, 7″ bowl, probably a crushed fruit bowl used with a metal lid notched for a spoon, probably 1930's.

189. Oval bowl, 4¾″ by 8″, maker unknown, probably 1930's.

190. Two of McKee's #37 Modernistic kitchen shakers, 4″ tall, initialed for salt and pepper, about 1930-1937; black ones were also lettered with the full names "Pepper" and "Sugar", and presumably "Salt" and "Flour". See also Figure 399.

191. 7½″ bowl, possibly McKee's #2 mixing bowl, circa 1931, in metal two-handled holder.

192. McKee Glass Company's Sunkist orange reamer, 8½″ long. Sunkist reamers were made by McKee 1926-1951, the scarce black examples probably in the 1930's. Made for growers only.

193. McKee's Bottoms-Up cocktail tumbler, 1932. This was made with the legs together (as shown), with a patent number molded near the rim; another variety, apparently also made by McKee, has the legs apart and lacks the patent number. There are other varieties, of unknown make, which are not found in black.

In 1979 appeared a new tumbler, made by Guernsey Glass Company, in colors including a dark brown approaching black. It is a copy of the McKee legs-together style, but lacks the patent marking on the McKee product.

194. 5″ pin tray, maker uncertain. This may be Dithridge and Company's #70, advertised on December 7, 1899; however, the advertisement does not show the details clearly, and there seems to be a similar heart-shaped tray of unknown make.

16

Continued On page 64

1

2

3

4

5   6   7

8   9   10   11A   11B   11C

12A   12C   12D   13   14

12B

15   16   17   18   19

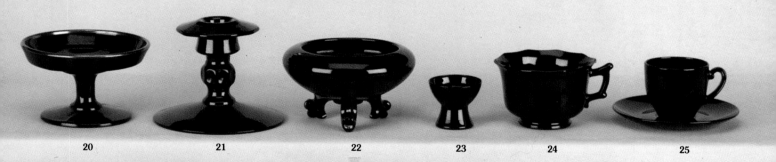

20   21   22   23   24   25

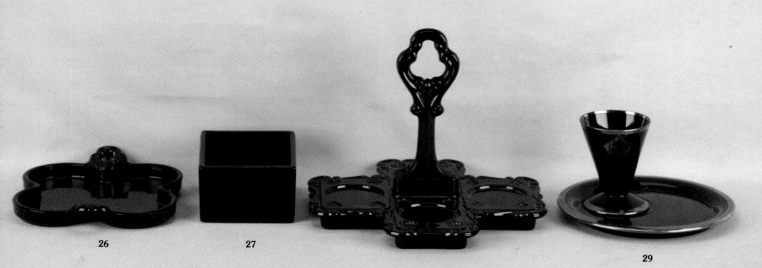

26   27   28   29

30   31   32   33

34   35   36

37A   37B   38   39   40

41   42   43   44

45   46   47   48

49   50   51   52   53

55   56   57

58   59   60   61

62   63   64   65

L.E. Smith and Greensburg

66   67   68   70A   70B

71   72   73   74   75   76A   76B   76C

77   78   79   81   82

80

23

83 84 85 86A 86B

87 88 89

90 91 92 93 94

95   96   97   98   99

100   101   102   103

104   105   106   107   108

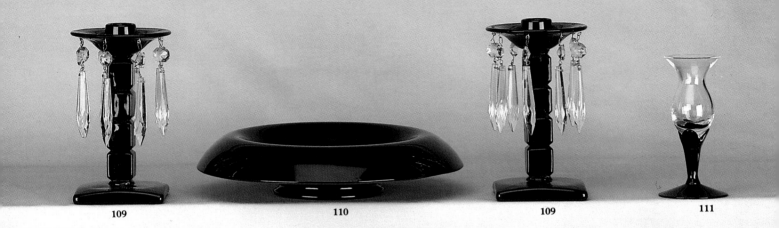

109   110   109   111

112   113   114   115

116   117   118

119   120   121   122   123

124   125   126A   126B

127   128   129

130

135A   135B   135C

131A   131B   132   133   134

141

136   137   138   139   140   142

143   144   145

Imperial,
et Cetera

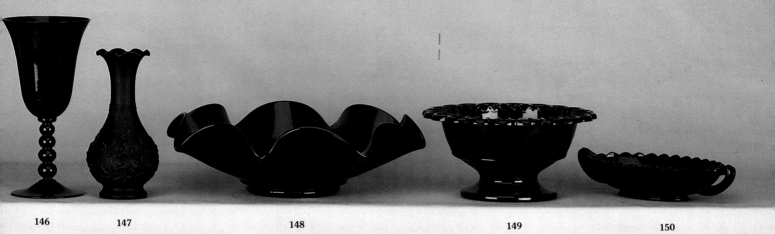

146   147   148   149   150

151   152   153A   153B   154

155   156   157   158   159

160   161   162   163

164   165   166   167   168

172

169   170   171

173   174   175

176 177 178 179 180

181   182   183

184   185   186   187

188   189   190   191

  192   193   194   195   196

New Martinsville,
et Cetera

197   198   199

200   201   202   203A   203B   204

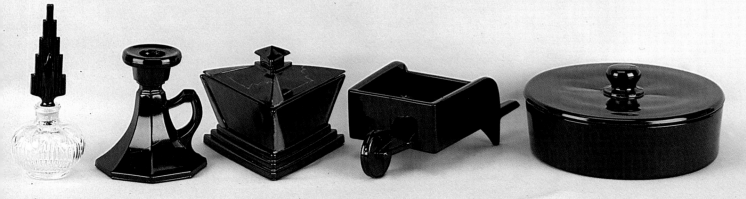

205   206   207   208   209   33

210   211   212   213   214

215   216   217   218

219   220   221

222   223   224   225

226   227   228

229   230   231   232

234

233

235A

235B

236

237

238

239

240

241

244

242

243

245

L.E. Smith and Others

246   247   248A   248B   249

250   251   252 A   252B

253   254   255   256   257

258   259   260   261

262   263   264   265

266   268   269   270

267

271

272

273

274

275

276

277

278

279

280

281

282

283   284   285

286   287   288   289

290   291   292   293   294

295   296   297   298   299   300A   300B

302

303

304

305

306

307

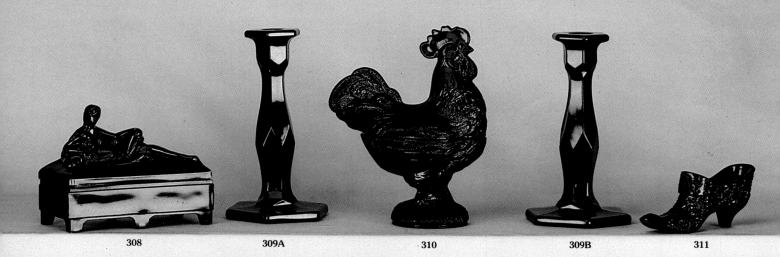

308 309A 310 309B 311

312 313 314 315 316

317 318 319 320

321   322   323   324   325   326   327   328

329   330   331   332   333

334   335   336   337   338   339   340

43

341   342   343   344   345   346   347

348   349   350   351   352

353   354   355   356   357   358   359   360

361   362   363   364   365

366   367   368   369   370

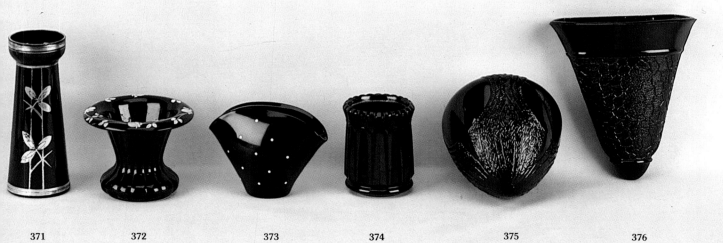

371   372   373   374   375   376

377   378   379   380   381   382

383   384   385   386   387

388   389   390   391   392   393

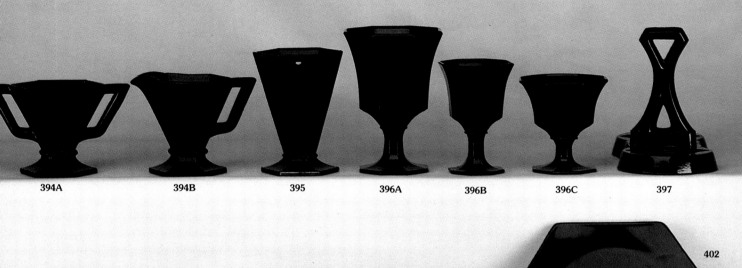

394A   394B   395   396A   396B   396C   397

402

398A   398B   399   400A   400B

401

403   404   405   406   408
                 407   409

410   411   412

413   514   415   416

417   418   419   420   421

422

48

423   424   425   426

429

427

428   430

431   432   433

434   435   436   437

439

438   440

50

441   442   443

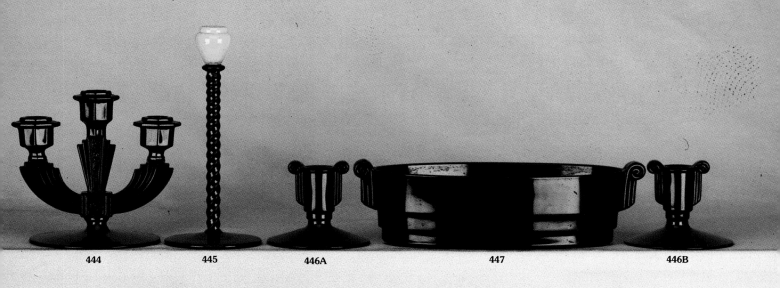

444   445   446A   447   446B

448   449   450   451

452   453   454   455   456   457

51

458   459   460

461   462   463

464   465   466

467   468   469   470   471

472

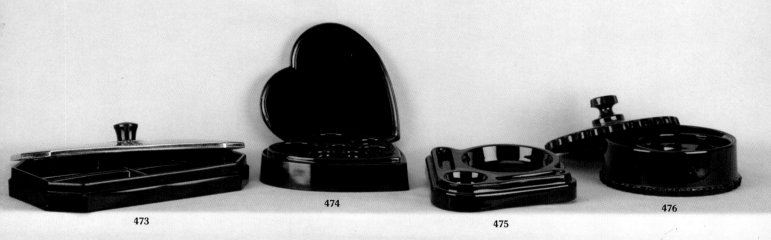

473   474   475   476

478   483

477   480   481   484   485   486

479   482   487

53

488   489   490

491   492   493   494

495   496   497   498   499   500

501   502   503   504   505   506

507   508   509A   509B   509C   510   511

516

514

517

512A

512B   519

513   515A   515B   518

55

520   521   522   523   524   525   526   527

528   529   530A   530C   530D

530B   531

534

532   533   536   537   539

535   538

540

541

542

543

544

545

546

547

548

549

550

551

552

553

554

555

556

57

557

558

559

560

561

562

563

564

565

566

567A

567B

567C

568   569   570   571   572

573   574   575   576   577

578   579   580   581   582   583

584   585   586   587   588

589   590   591   592   593   594

595   596   597   598

60

599
600
601
602

603
604
605
606
607
608
609

610
611
612
613
614
615
616

617
618
619
620
621
622

61

623 624 625 626 627 628 629 630 631

632 633 634 635 636 637 638

639 640 641 642 643 644 645 646 647

648 649 650 651 652 653 654 655 656 657

658

659

Continued From page 16

195. 11¼" comb and brush tray, probably made by Pittsburg Lamp, Brass and Glass Company, as it appears in 1906 and 1907 Butler Brothers wholesale groups of decorated opaque glass which include items formerly made by Dithridge and Company before it merged into the Pittsburg Company.

196. Heart jewel box, 3½". This item was made by McKee and Brothers and presumably by their successors, National Glass Company and McKee-Jeannette Glass Works, 1899-1907, in milk-white and clear glass. Since the late 1950's it has been made in many colors by Crystal Art Glass, since about 1972 with molded trademarks on the base. The date and maker of this black example are uncertain.

197. Maker unknown, 10½" 2 handled sandwich plate. Plates of this shape were decorated by Lotus Glass Company about 1931, but the etching on this one is unidentified. See also Figure 490.

198. Viking Glass Company's #974-1S swan-neck dish, or bon-bon with swan handle, 5¼", ebony with clear neck and head, 1950.

199. Viking's swan-neck bowl, 12", 1950.

200-203B. New Martinsville Glass Manufacturing Company's Addie* pattern pieces, 1930-probably 1931: (200) cup and saucer, (201) salad plate, (202) cup and saucer, (203A) sugar, (203B) cream. 202 and 203A and B are decorated with an unidentified etching featuring a pair of poppy blossoms.

204. Viking Glass Company's #772 flower cart, probably 1940's, possibly also made before 1944 by New Martinsville Glass Company.

205. Bottle, clear with black stopper, of the #25 Jerry* vanity set made by New Martinsville Glass Company at some time in the period 1937-1944.

206. Hot Shot* handled candlestick, maker unknown, possibly 1920's. It has been said that this was made by Federal Glass Company; Federal does not appear to have made black glass.

207. Triad* powder box, maker uncertain, with gold decoration. A 1924 patent for a similar design is associated with New Martinsville Glass Manufacturing company, which made in the early 1930's a light jade green similar to that found in Triad. A smaller sugar and cream in this pattern are known, but not a cream of a size to match this piece. Another name for Triad is Pyramid*, which is much better known as the name of another pattern.

208. #737 wheelbarrow, made at the same factory as the items in Figures 198-205, reportedly while it was operated by New Martinsville Glss Company, 1937-1944.

209. New Martinsville Glass Manufacturing Company's #10 candy box and cover, circa 1926.

Figures 210-221: **L. E. Smith Glass Company.**

210. #1900 flared top, 2 handled, footed vase, height 7¼", shown in a 1930's catalogue.·

211. #102, described as "Fancy 2 Handled Vase Black with Silver Dec.", in an L. E. Smith catalogue of the 1930's. This vase with slightly different silver decoration was among items sold to F. W. Woolworth Company.

212. Urn vase, 7¾" high, reportedly late 1920's-1930's, with original L. E. Smith label.

213. Snake Dance* #433 crimped top, two handled, footed vase, reportedly made 1928-1932, sold at one time to F. W. Woolworth Co. The same shape without the molded panel of dancers was #433 on some Smith catalogue pages.

214. Vase, Greensburg Glass Works' #1016, about early 1930's, with unidentified silver decoration.

215. #9/4 window box, about 1930-1935, shown in a 'Special Listing with F. W. Woolworth Co.'; pictured here with an apparently original flower block.

216. #2 3-footed jardiniere, silver decorated as offered by Smith, with flower block, probably 1930's. Often called Greek Key.

217. Fern bowl #1, shown in catalogues of about 1930-1935.

218. Footed Hobnail ivy ball, #85, 5" high, about early 1930's.

219. Greensburg Glass Works' #181 handled tumbler tray, 8" diameter, about late 1920's-early 1930's, holding four footed tumblers, maker unknown, each with clear bowl decorated in color with a rooster, depicted in a different position on each tumbler.

220. Jardiniere, sometimes called Bluebird*, probably made by L. E. Smith: compare Figures 216 and 217.

221. Greek Key Bean Pot, silver decorated, with lid which doubles as a center-handled tray; probably made by L. E. Smith in the late 1920's or early 1930's. Handles very similar to, or matching, this center handle are found on Smith pieces.

The pieces in Figures 222-232, except Figure 225, were made by **L. E. Smith Glass Company** about 1930-1935. There is some confusion in regard to pattern names. This is due in part to the fact that some shapes can be found with or without the embossed "shield" design seen here in Figures 222, 224, 229, and 230. While some writers would call all of these Smith items Mount Pleasant*, the classification used here seems somewhat more logical.

222. Double Shield* #600 double candleholder.

223. Mount Pleasant 2½" candlestick.

224. Do-Si-Do* #410 salad bowl, 8½".

225. Maker unknown, handled tray with silver decoration, about early 1930's.

226. Mount Pleasant two handled salad tray.

227. Mount Pleasant saucer, 6½".

228. Mount Pleasant plate, about 8".

229. Mount Pleasant 3 footed triangle bowl, 3".

230. Mount Pleasant #327 cupped bowl.

231. Mount Pleasant #515 footed cupped bowl.

232. Mount Pleasant #525 3 footed flared bowl or bon bon dish, 3", with silver bands probably applied by L. E. Smith.

Figures 233-245: **L. E. Smith Glass Company,** about 1930-1935, except as noted.

233. Do-Si-Do* two-handled cake plate, 9½".

234. #65 cocktail tray, also sold in a dresser set, 1932.

235A and B. Mount Pleasant* sugar and creamer.

236. Mount Pleasant cup and saucer.

237. Do-Si-Do plate, about 8".

238. Mount Pleasant sherbet, 3".

239. Maker unknown, 7½" plate, about 1930-1935.

240. #200 handled nut or tray, 5½" diameter.

241. Mount Pleasant three-footed plate.

242. #200 mayonnaise bowl and #200 mayonnaise plate, 7".

243. Two-handled plate with two sides rolled up, 7".

244. Maker unknown, salt and pepper shakers, hgt. 4½", probably 1925-1935.

245. Mount Pleasant #505 one handled nut, 9" diameter.

The date of the type of white decoration on black glass shown by Figures 246-249 and 252A has been variously given, as 1928-1932 by Stout (*DG* 3, pp. 20, 21), and as the 1940's and early 1950's by Weatherman, who attributes it to L. E. Smith Glass Company (in Koch 1, p. Weatherman 14). The latter period seems more likely for most of the items here. Stout calls this decoration Veined Onyx*.

246. Footed urn with cover, by L. E. Smith. Compare Figure 212.

247. Cake salver, 4½" by 10", by L. E. Smith. A distributor advertised a milk-white (?) square compote in this pattern in 1972, along with a Smith item.

248A and B. Sugar and creamer which appear to be in Hazel-Atlas Glass Company's Ovide* pattern.

249. Crimped compote, 7" by 9", matching Figure 247, by L. E. Smith.

250. Paden City Glass Manufacturing Company's Nada* pattern footed ivy ball, 4½", probably 1930-1935. This pattern is distinguished by the square shape and scalloped rim of most pieces, features difficult to recognize in this cupped piece. Other names for the pattern are Vaara*, Mrs. "B"*, and Avis*.

251. L. E. Smith's #50 bulb bowl, about 1930-1935.

252A and B. Decorated and plain examples of a 3½" by 7½" footed salver, undoubtedly from the same manufacturer as Figures 247 and 249.

253. Napkin holder, maker uncertain, 4" high, 4" long, probably late 1920's-mid-1930's, in a design similar to Paden City's #210 Mowgli* (also known as Regina*) pattern.

254. Snake Dance* salt shaker and pepper shaker, height 3½", by L. E. Smith in the period 1928-1932. Other pattern names: Dancing Ladies and Pan*.

255. L. E. Smith's Snake Dance #404 window box, sold with a flower block shaped to rest in the top, about 1931-1935, shown here with decorated top rim.

256. Vase, height 6", maker unknown, probably late 1920's-mid-1930's.

257. L. E. Smith's #711 vase, height 6", silver decorated, about 1930-1935.

Figures 258-270: **L. E. Smith Glass Company,** about 1930-1935, except as noted.

258. Triangle vase, pattern number unknown, in molded design like Smith's #1931 vase, but with a scalloped edge similar to that of Mount Pleasant*.

259. #432/5 fancy crimped top 2 handled footed vase.

260. #432 crimped vase, silver decorated by Smith.

261. #1000 cupped vase. See also Figure 68.

262. #49 crimped vase, silver decorated by Smith.

263. #2400 2 handled footed bon bon dish, height 3".

264. #2400 2 handled footed fruit bowl, height 4½".

265. #800 Garland* footed urn vase.

266. 6" 3-footed bowl, pattern number unknown. This design in a 9" size was Smith's #1022 console bowl.

267. Greensburg Glass Works' #8 Vermiculate* flower block, 4¾", about late 1920's-early 1930's. has matching pattern vase.

268. 4" flower pot and saucer, pattern number unknown, matching Smith's #201 3" flower pot and saucer.

269. Flower bowl, 6½" diameter, probably made by L. E. Smith, which made several Hobnail pieces, including a #77 violet bowl very similar to this piece.

270. #2-H fern bowl (H probably standing for Hobnail) and #4 flower block.

The following black satin-finish glassware, Figures 271-282, except Figure 274, was made by **United States Glass Company,** probably at its Factory R in Tiffin, Ohio.

271. #9574 basket, catalogued as 6" (probably referring to width of opening), 1926.

272. #310 Chatham open work comport, 8½" per catalogue, diameter of mouth 5", 1926-1927. This pattern has also been named Bowman*.

273. #66 Twist* candlestick, 8", 1926. Notice the ridges next to the bold rid spiraling around the stem. Cambridge Glass Company evidently made about 1923 a candlestick of nearly identical design, which also has these ridges. Reportedly Cambridge examples have two vertical mold seam lines while those from United States Glass have three. Another type lacks the spiral ridges, and is of uncertain origin.

274. Bud vase, possibly H. C. Fry Glass Company's #804, about 1929-1933, decorated with gold lines; however, Cambridge's #2355 and #276, Standard Glass Manufacturing Company's #150 (or #250), and Bartlett-Collins Company's #375 are very similar shapes. (Bartlett-Collins probably did not make black glass.) See also Figure 367.

275. #315 (or #15315) high foot comport, 7½" (diameter) per catalogue, 7" high, 1926.

276. #8076 Leeds or Old Leedsware orange bowl, 1926, with separate base, 1926, one of two bases on which it was displayed in United States Glass Company advertising. Other firms made bases very similar to this one. Satin-finished black bases are scarce. Westmoreland Glass Company's #1891 Spoke and Rim bowl with attached foot, made in black in 1954 and later, is very similar.

277. Candlestick in #151 (earlier, #15151) Pompeian* pattern, 1926; this shape is also known as Skirted Base* candlestick.

278. Probably United States Glass Company's #179 (earlier, #15179) console bowl, circa 1929. This was offered with a base similar to the one in Figure 276, but in a smaller size.

279. #310 Chatham open work bonbon, 3″ high, circa 1927.

280. #9298 Stag ash tray, 5¾″ by 4¾″, 1926, reportedly designed by Reuben Haley.

281. #15179 (or #179) low footed comport or urn, 4½″ by 4″ high, with gold lines on edges, circa 1925. Has matching compote.

282. #320 (or #15320) wall vase, 9¾″, circa 1927.

Figures 283-293: **United States Glass Company,** except as noted.

283. #16255 Poppy vase, made by United States Glass, 1930, possibly at Glassport, Pennsylvania; satin finished; decorated with tiny bits of glass, applied possibly by McCourt Studios, Minneapolis.

284. Three-footed salver, 11½″, also found in a 12½″ size, reportedly made by United States Glass, circa 1926. The underside is shown here.

285. Shaggy Daisy* three-footed salver, 10″, 1930.

286. #8098 footed console bowl in United States Glass' Satin Ribbon etched decoration, about mid-1920's. The base is one piece with the bowl.

287. Rolled edge console bowl, maker unknown, in frosted or satin finish with gold decoration matching that in Figure 288. Bowls of similar shape were made by many manufacturers.

288. Candlestick, maker uncertain, in satin finish with unidentified gold decoration. Candlesticks of this approximate shape in various colors were United States Glass' #10, 1925-1927 and probably to 1929; Cambridge Glass Company's #227½, 1927-1930; Fenton Art Glass Company's #314, circa 1925; Paden City Glass Manufacturing Company's #118, probably mid- or late 1920's; Bartlett-Collins Company's #87 (probably not made in black), circa 1927; and reportedly Duncan and Miller Glass Company's #35.

289. Bowl or vase, 6½″ by 4¾″ high, clear and black. This specific item is not documented as a United States Glass Company product except by the Tiffin label on it, but it is very similar in design to pieces made by this firm, including some advertised in 1959. It may have been made by one of the succeeding Tiffin firms after 1962.

290. #15320 (also catalogued as #320 and #330)

handled cake plate or sandwich tray, 1927-1929, with etched Satin Ribbon decoration.

291. #16256 floral design vase with molded poppies, in satin finish, 1930, reportedly made at Glassport, Pennsylvania. This was also available with a matching lid, for use as a bath salts jar.

292. #16254 vase with floral design (molded Iris), 1932. Made like #291.

293. #12 low candleholder, 1926-1927, apparently made at Tiffin, Ohio; with unidentified floral decoration.

294. Bud vase, probably H. C. Fry Glass Company's #809 shape decorated by Fry, 1929-1933.

295 and 296. Rose and Thorn* pattern small and large nappies, reportedly made by United States Glass Company, probably in the early 1930's.

297. 8-ounce goblet, clear with black foot, maker unknown, probably of the period 1929-1935.

298. Footed tumbler, clear with black foot, maker unknown, from about 1929-1935.

299. Octagon Scroll* cup, made by United States Glass Company, reportedly in 1930, and a saucer not matching the cup, but similar to Figure 171.

300A and B. Octagon Scroll sugar and cream, United States Glass, circa 1930. This pattern has also been called simply Octagon* and Scroll*. Has matching pattern on bottom of saucer.

301. 9″ tray, New Martinsville Glass Manufacturing Company. This style of tray was used in the #149 Allah smoker's set, which included also a cigarette holder and two ash trays; the known 1925 advertising for this set offers several colors, but not black. The black tray has been found in a dresser set combining black with jade, which probably dates from the early 1930's.

302. Flared bowl, 10½″, maker unknown, probably 1920's.

303. Flared cupped bowl, 7″, possibly Fenton Art Glass Company's #640, circa 1921-1925.

304. Bowl, 10″, maker unknown, probably 1920's.

305. Center-handled tray, 8½″, possibly made by L. E. Smith Glass Company (see discussion under Figure 149). This tray with the rim flat rather than turned up was advertised in milk-white in 1953.

306. Plate, maker unknown. Reportedly this was made by Indiana Glass Company in 1936, but the black and dark blue in which it is found are not among Indiana's known colors of that era. Westmoreland Glass Company made a plate of very similar pattern, which apparently does not have the circular footrim seen here. The plate here has been called Maple Leaf*, a name also used for many other pressed glass items.

307. Westmoreland Glass Company's #1902 dresser set or bath set, consisting of two 4½″ bottles, a 4″ puff box, and a 10″ tray, date uncertain. This set appears in other colors in Westmoreland catalogues of circa 1971-1977, usually with the lips of the bottles shaped differently than shown here. A few other #1902 items were made as early as the 1920's. See also Figures 568 and 582.

308. 8″ box with figure of reclining woman on cover, maker unknown, possibly 1930-1935.

309A and B. Pair of 8¼″ candlesticks, maker unknown, probably 1920's.

Figures 310-320: **Westmoreland Glass Company,** except as noted.

310. #6 Standing Rooster or simply Rooster, a covered dish 8½″ tall, with Westmoreland mark inside head, made in black in 1955. This is also known as Pedestal Rooster* and Tall Rooster*. Reportedly this was copied from a dish made in France, and a recent copy has been imported from Taiwan; neither seems to exist in black. Some Westmoreland examples, at least in milk-white, are unmarked.

311. Slipper, 6″ long, probably L. E. Smith Glass Company's #80, made in milk-white in 1969 or earlier, in clear glass in 1982-1983; black examples may be from the 1950's.

312. #1000, 1000 Eye line, Turtle cigarette box, 7½″ long, 1949-circa 1953 and reportedly mid-1960's. Several much older patterns have become known as Thousand Eye*, but were not so named by the manufacturers, as this was. The Westmoreland design has sometimes been called Hundred Eye*, and this item simply Black Turtle*.

313. #456 Lady candy bowl, 9″ long, circa 1953-1954.

314. #1820 three piece individual salt and pepper set, 1930, in clear and black.

315. Mayonnaise ladle, 5″ long, possibly Westmoreland's. This or a very similar ladle appears as #1800 in a catalogue of about 1928, but as #1837 in a catalogue of about 1967.

316. #1921 Lotus candy, circa 1967-1971. The same piece but with the bowl shallower was made in the 1920's as a honey (which may not have been made in black). Figures 112, 572, and 575 show other pieces of this pattern.

317. New Martinsville Glass Manufacturing Company's Judy* puff box, 1930, in clear with black cover.

318. #1 toy pistol, 5″ long, circa 1973. Also made in 1913 with different end on barrel.

319. #1211 Doreen* (other name: Pam*) 3″ candlestick, 1930, satin finished, with painted flowers and gilt edges.

320. #6 Three Owls plate, 7″, with Westmoreland mark on back, circa 1949-1954.

321 and 322. 8-ounce footed tumbler and 6-ounce fruit salad, probably belonging to a Liberty Works line of 1930, with an unidentified light cutting.

323. 8-ounce footed tumbler with ten-scalloped foot, probably part of Seneca Glass Company's Allegheny* line, 1931. See also Figure 325.

324. 4-ounce sherbet with eight-scalloped foot, probably of Louie Glass Company's #3850 line, 1930, or a very similar H. C. Fry Glass Company line of the same year. See also Figure 326.

325. 12-ounce footed tumbler with ten-scalloped foot, probably Seneca's Allegheny (see Figure 323).

326. 12-ounce footed tumbler with eight-scalloped foot, possibly matching Figure 324.

327. 8-ounce footed tumbler, maker unknown, probably late 1920's-mid-1930's, with unidentified cutting.

328. 1-ounce cordial, maker unknown, probably after 1928.

329. Cologne (?) bottle with stopper, in shape of elephant and rider, possibly made in Europe about 1920-1940; height 7″, length 4½″.

330. Co-Operative Flint Glass Company's Elephant covered dish in the smaller size. See discussion under Figure 4.

331. Westmoreland Glass Company's #81 Hi-Hat, about late 1920's.

332. United States Glass Company's Canoe, 6¼″ long, reportedly made 1924-1936, often found with souvenir lettering, at least some of which was applied by United States Glass. This one is marked as a souvenir of Cheyenne, Wyoming, and gilded on the rim. This shape has been called Boat Salt*, but other items fit that description, and it is doubtful this one was intended for salt. Another name is Canoe Souvenir*.

333. Two-handled 8″ footed bowl, maker uncertain. A dish of somewhat similar design, with handles matching these, was registered by the English firm of George Davidson and Company in 1937.

334. 10″ tray, possibly in the same pattern as New Martinsville Glass Company's #38 three part celery and relish, 9″ per catalogues, which has a different rim. Available records show #38 as made by this firm under this 1937-1944 name and the later name Viking Glass Company; the pattern number suggests that it was introduced about 1933 by the New Martinsville Glass Manufacturing Company.

335. Paper-cup holder, resembling a footed tumbler but with a hole in the bottom, 4¼″ high, marked "VeeCup" on bottom, maker unknown, possibly 1925-1935. This and other matching sizes and shapes (see Figure 337) are attributed to Vortex, probably not a glass manufacturer.

336. Shell-shaped dish with gold edge, 5¾″, maker and date unknown.

337. Paper-cup holder, probably for ice cream, 2½″ high, matching Figure 335.

338. Footed individual salt, 1¾″ high, maker uncertain. Very similar salts were made in two companies' lines: Cambridge Glass Company's #2630 (sometimes called Cambridge's Colonial, Paul Revere or Plymouth, one of which may have been the original name) and #2750 Colonial (or Nearcut Colonial*) about 1910-1917, and Duncan and Miller Glass Company's #61 Polished Panels* (other names: Sweet Sixty-One* and Late Colonial, Variant*) and #65 Charleston (other name: Polished Mirror*), about 1909-1913.

339. Maker unknown, 6-ounce egg glass. Virtually this shape was Cambridge's #952 and #954 (circa 1903-1910), Duncan and Miller's #910 (circa 1909), McKee Glass Company's #910 (about 1920), and probably was made by other firms.

340. Imperial Glass Corporation's Chesterfield* salt dip, made in black circa 1966, when four of these made up an SD6 salt dip set. Earlier this shape was included in Imperial Glass Company's #600 pattern. Other names: Zak*, Flute*, Colonial*, Pee Wee*.

341. Witches Pot*, 3¼″ high, probably made in England between 1860 and 1900. The intended use of this piece is uncertain; a smaller version is said to have been a salt.

342. Dalzell, Gilmore and Leighton Company's Crown* tall footed lamp, crystal with ebony foot, 10″, one of several sizes made, circa 1897.

343. Eagle Glass and Manufacturing Company's Starbright* vase, 6″ tall, circa 1899.

344-347. Four vases, with enameled (two also with gilt) decoration, in styles typical of many imported from Austria-Hungary in the late 19th and early 20th centuries.

348. Cow On Round Base* covered dish, 6½″. The likely date is between 1875 and 1910. It has been said that this was made in France. A similar lid was later made in several colors by Kemple Glass Works, which used it on a different style of base.

349. Jug embossed with tavern scene, height 5″, European, probably late 19th or early 20th century.

350. Cream jug, 4″ high, European, possibly English, about 1870-1890.

351. United States Glass Company base for a fish bowl, 6½″ by 3″ high, satin-finished, possibly 1928.

352. Satin-finished comport, 5½″ tall, 5¾″ across, decorated with gold and red, origin unknown, probably 1915-1930.

353. Paperweight or ornament, 5″, embossed "HERRENHAUS bei STEINSCHOENAU". The German form of the latter name suggests a date before World War I; the Bohemian glassmaking center Steinschoenau is now Kamenický Senov, Czechoslovakia.

354. Half Scroll* match holder, maker unknown, probably 1900-1910.

355. Boot with spur, possibly a match holder, 3″, maker uncertain, about 1875-1895. This has been attributed to the Pennsylvania firm of Challinor, Taylor and Company; it has also been considered English, and so named British Boot*. Two varieties are found in old examples, those having a deep indentation in the sole said to be Challinor's. A copy made in several colors in recent years by Mosser Glass, Inc., is called #262 Cowboy Boot.

356. Bee* toothpick vase, 2½″ square, maker uncertain, circa 1887; also called Gold Fly*, Bee*, Bees on a Basket*, Bees-in-a-Basket*. The last two names are used also for another item resembling this, but having a handle and other differences.

357. Shoe-shaped bottle, 5¼″, 3⅓″ high, made for a screw cap, maker unknown, possibly 1880-1910.

358. Hollow blown egg, 3½″ by 2½″, with gilded Easter decoration, maker unknown, probably 1895-1910.

359. Tumbler (?), 10-ounce, maker unknown, possibly 1915-1925.

360. Toothpick or match box, probably the Saratoga Hat offered by Cambridge Glass Company in 1903; the black examples were probably made earlier by one of the firms which merged to form Cambridge's parent, National Glass Company. Very similar items were made by others; the Cambridge type, which has a bow on the hatband, may have been the only one made in black.

361. Square vase, 7¾″ tall, maker unknown, probably 1930's.

362. Crimped vase, 10″, maker unknown, about 1927-1935.

363. Bottle vase, 10½″ tall, maker and date unknown.

364. Vase, 15″ tall, decorated with bird on branch in silver, probably made in Czechoslovakia about 1920-1935.

365. Decanter, 15½″ tall, maker unknown, probably after 1920.

366. Epergne, 7½″ diameter, 9¾″ high, maker unknown, possibly 1915-1930.

367. See Figure 274. This is the same shape, differing only in gold decoration.

368. Vase, 9½″, with gold decoration, Czechoslovakian (marked), probably 1920's. Vases of similar shape were made in the United States: Bryce Brothers Company's #1 and #2, and probably others.

369. A different enamel decoration on the same shape shown in Figure 294, which see for further information.

370. Vase, height 7¼″, maker unknown, probably 1930's.

371. Hyacinth vase, 6″, with silver decoration, possibly Czechoslovakian, probably 1920's.

372. Vase, 3″, with white enamel flowers, maker unknown, probably 1915-1935.

373. Vase, 3″, with white enamel dots, maker unknown, probably 1925-1935.

374. Match safe (?), height 3½″, possibly 1900-1930.

375. Vase, 5″, apparently to be used in metal hanger; possibly matching Greensburg Glass Works' #1012 flower bowl, about 1930.

376. Wall vase, 5¾″, possibly made in the 1920's by United States Glass Company, which made a very similar wall vase in 1927 and about 1957. This pattern appears to match the carnival glass items known as Crackle*, but it is not clear if this is from the same maker. Another name for the design is Tree of Life*, unsatisfactory because it is also used for other patterns.

377. Vase, 9″ tall, maker unknown, possibly 1915-1930.

378. Vase, 9″ tall, possibly H. P. Sinclaire and Company's #3354, about 1923.

379. Cambridge Glass Company's Community #2800/113 9″ vase, about 1916-1920.

380. Vase, 10½″ tall, maker unknown, probably 1915-1930.

381. Vase, height 9¼″, maker uncertain, probably 1915-1930. Steuben Glass Works and/or Steuben Division of Corning Glass Works made virtually this shape, in other sizes, before 1933; also compare the next item.

382. Vase, height 7½″, probably Greensburg Glass Works' #1019, about 1930.

383. Cuspidor, 6¾″ by 4½″ high, maker unknown, probably 1915-1935. Cuspidors differing slightly in shape were United States Glass Company's (#9441?), which was offered in black, Cambridge Glass Company's Community #2800/215, and probably others.

384. Vase, 5¾″ tall, maker unknown, probably 1915-1930.

385. Vase, 8″ tall, probably H. C. Fry Glass Company's #811, about 1929.

386, 387. Ladies Spittoons, small (for dresser) & large 6″ by 4½″ high and 8″ by 6¼″ high, maker unknown, possibly 1925-1940.

388. Vase, 4½″, maker unknown, possibly 1925-1940.

389. Vase, 4½″, maker unknown, probably 1915-1925.

390. Vase, 6″, maker unknown, probably 1915-1935.

391. Vase, 5½″, probably made by Paden City Glass Manufacturing Company. The same shape is found with Paden City's #515 Lela Bird* etching, which was new in 1929. The painted decoration here is of unknown origin.

392. Vase or candlestick, 5″ tall, maker unknown, probably after 1930.

393. Vase, 7¼″, maker unknown, possibly 1925-1940.

394A and B. Sugar and cream, six-sided, maker unknown, probably 1924-1935.

395. Footed tumbler, 5″, matching 394 A and B.

396A, B, C. Goblet, wine, and sherbet in an eight-sided pattern, maker unknown, probably after 1970.

397. Art Deco tray for sugar and creamer, made by Indiana Glass for Tiara Exclusives, circa 1973. See also Figure 592.

398A and B. Fostoria Glass Company's #2375½ Fairfax tea sugar and tea cream, probably made in the 1929-1941 period. See also Figures 117 and 118.

399. Two of McKee Glass Company's kitchen shakers, lettered S and P in a different style than Figure 190, (see for further information).

400A and B. Sugar and cream, maker unknown, probably 1926-1935.

401 and 402. Cup and saucer and 8″ plate, matching Figures 394 and 395.

403. Hazel-Atlas Glass Company's Moderntone pepper and salt, 4″ tall, possibly 1934 or 1935. This pattern is well known in dark blue, amethyst, and opaque white decorated with various colors, but unrecorded in black. One metal top is probably not original. Another name for the pattern is Wedding Band*.

404. Two of Paden City Glass Manufacturing Company's #210 Regina* small shakers with probably original metal tops, 3″ tall, about 1929-1935.

405. Bowl, 6¼″ diameter, maker unknown, probably 1920-1930.

406. Candy jar lacking cover, maker uncertain, probably 1928-1935. This has been considered part of Hocking Glass Company's Block Optic pattern (see Figure 137), which it closely resembles, but Hocking is not known to have made black.

407. Plate, 6⅛″, maker unknown, probably 1920-1935.

408. Jerri* cup, maker unknown, probably 1928-1935.

409. Saucer, 5¾″, in a design similar to Figure 407.

410. Cannister with aluminum cover, 8″ high, maker unknown, probably 1930's.

411. Tub, 8½″ by 6″ high, date uncertain. This originally bore a label identifying the contents as syrup for restaurant use.

412. Sugar (?) cannister with embossed S and aluminum cover, 8″ high, maker unknown, probably 1930's.

413. Westmoreland Glass Company twine holder, 3″ by 3″, date uncertain. This item was offered, apparently in all clear glass, in 1973; this or a very similar twine holder was #1860 in a Westmoreland catalogue of about 1925-1929.

414. Jar with stopper, 6½″ tall, marked on bottom "Container Made In Belgium," probably made after 1960; possibly sold containing a bath or cosmetic product.

415. Tea warmer, 5″ by 4″ high, maker unknown, possibly 1930's. A small cup or wax pot holding a candle sits underneath this to heat a tea pot placed on top.

416. Store display tray, 9″ by 6½″, embossed "CLARKS TEABERRY GUM" on the front, maker unknown, possibly 1920-1940.

417. Mixing bowl, 5″, possibly Hazel-Atlas Glass Company's #773, circa 1929.

418. Egg cup (shown upside down), clear glass with black enamel on base, 4¼″ tall, maker unknown, probably 1930's.

419. Jar with lid, 4″ tall, lettered "Hengstenberg" and decorated in rust and green; maker unknown, probably after 1960.

420. Cheese (?) dish with clear glass cover, 5″ diameter, maker unknown, possibly 1925-1940.

421. Marked Sunbeam CFS CO CHICAGO USA, this 4″ by 6″ piece appears to be the base of a mixer or other kitchen appliance.

422. Hand formed item of solid glass, 14½″ long, probably made before 1880. While similar items are usually referred to as rolling pins, it has been reported that pieces with stubby knob ends like this were used as towel bars, either hung by cord or in a wooden frame.

423. Ebon* design VeeCup paper cup holder, 5¼″ tall. See also Figures 335 and 337.

424. 10-ounce footed tumbler, 6½″ tall, possibly Cambridge Glass Company's #7966, 1950.

425. Sandwich tray, 10½″, maker unknown, probably 1923-1940.

426. Daisy and Cube* 8-ounce goblet, 6″ tall, with the Black Forest etching, made for L. G. Wright Glass Company, probably by Viking Glass Company, about 1974-1975. Daisy and Cube was the #600 pattern of Bellaire Goblet Company, circa 1886-1891, continued by Bellaire's successor, United States Glass Company, to about 1893. It may be that no goblet was then made in this pattern, nor was any black glass. Daisy and Cube is also known as Stars and Bars, a name of another pattern. Black Forest etching was first made about 1929-1931, for Frank L. Van Deman and Son, a New York sales firm. Its maker in those years is unknown, but the pieces on which it was etched at that time, in black and other colors, do not resemble Daisy and Cube.

427. 16-ounce tumbler, maker unknown, probably 1930's or later.

428. 8″ plate, maker unknown, probably after 1923.

429. 6″ dish, maker unknown, probably 1930-1960.

430. Grill plate, 9″, maker uncertain. A very similar 9½″ plate is reported to have been made in pink and green by United States Glass Company in the late 1920's.

431. 10″ plate, probably part of Imperial Glass Company's or Corporation's Molly* #727 cheese and cracker set (plate and a small comport), probably early 1930's. See also Figures 169, 171, 172, and 491.

432. Tray, 10½″ long, maker unknown, probably 1925-1940.

433. 10″ plate, maker unknown, probably 1920-1940. This plate, with a small comport (similar to Figure 20) standing on its center, probably composed a cheese and cracker set.

434. Console bowl, 11″, maker unknown, probably 1930's.

435 and 436. Bowls, 8″ and 4″, with different styles of metal feet; maker(s) unknown, probably 1930-1960.

437. Bowl, 9″, maker and date unknown.

438. Cupped bowl, 7″, possibly Fenton Art Glass Company's #2007, circa 1921.

439. Bowl, 11″, possibly United States Glass Company's #15179 orange bowl, about 1924-1935, with gold line decoration. See also Figures 278 and 281.

440. Bowl, 9¾″, with white enamel edge; maker uncertain, though H. Northwood Company has been suggested. This bowl was also made in stretch glass, in which it or a very similar bowl was advertised in 1925.

441. Footed bowl, 9″, twelve-sided, maker unknown, probably 1924-1935.

442. L. E. Smith Glass Company's #100 Romanesque* octagon bowl, about late 1920's-mid-1930's. This pattern is also known as Gothic Arch(es)*, and reportedly was advertised in the 1920's as Lace Renaissance*.

443. Lancaster Glass Company's #1831/7 tray, 10″, about 1931.

444. Three-light candelabrum, 7″ across, 6½″ high, made by United States Glass Company, probably in the 1930's.

445. Candlestick with opaque yellow cup, 9″ tall, maker unknown, possibly 1915-1930.

446A, B and 447. Fostoria Glass Company's #2443 4″ candlesticks and 10″ oval bowl, about 1931-1933.

448. Two-light candlestick, 6½″, maker unknown, probably 1930's.

449. Flossie* two-light candlestick, 4¾″ high, maker unknown, probably 1930-1950.

450. McKee Glass Company's #157 Scallop Edge rolled edge candlestick, 2″ high, probably early 1930's. See also Figure 184.

451. Three-light candlestick, 7½″ across, 4″ high, maker unknown, probably 1930-1960.

452. Candlestick, 2½″, maker unknown, probably 1930-1960.

453. Low candlestick, 3″, maker and date uncertain. Indiana Glass Company's #10 low candlestick, made circa 1940, appears to differ only in having a flatter foot and a different top rim.

454. Candlestick, 2½″, said to be part of Hazel-Atlas Glass Company's Ovide* pattern (see Figures 131A, B, 140-142, 248A, B). This piece has been given the name Pete and Repete*.

455. Candleholder, 3¼″ by 1½″, maker unknown, probably after 1935.

456. Base, 2½″ high, for group of glass flowers on wire stems, possibly 1925-1935.

457. Candleholder, 2½″. No marking. However, clear glass candleholders like this, embossed "TAIWAN" on the bottom, are for sale new at this writing.

458. Backward C* 9″ plate, probably made by L. E. Smith Glass Company, possibly in the 1950's, with Veined Onyx* white decoration. This decoration is discussed in connection with Figures 246-249 and 252A. The Backward C design was first made much earlier (see Figure 466), but apparently not in this size. Fenton Art Glass Company's #9019 9″ "C" plate, made in several colors in the years 1952-1961, is substantially the same in design, but on close comparison with the one here can be seen to have differently shaped openings in the rim. Fenton's is not known to have been made in black.

459. Gothic and Chain Border* 8″ plate, maker unknown, probably 1890's.

460. 8½″ Square "S" Border* plate, reportedly made by Canton Glass Company. This plate in three sizes, in black and milk white, was advertised under the name Minerva* by a wholesale firm in 1898. The same design in 8½″ size has been made by Westmoreland Glass Company, reportedly as early as the 1920's. Westmoreland had definitely made it in milk-white by 1949, and in that year offered it in black. Other sizes in milk-white were reported on the market in the 1930's and 1940's; what factory or factories were making them is unknown. Minerva is the accepted name of another pattern.

461. Wickerwork* 9″ plate, made by the English firm Sowerby's Ellison Glass Works Ltd., whose trademark it bears. In other colors, this design was probably being made in the latter half of the 1920's, but may also have been made as early as the 1870's; the date of black glass examples is uncertain.

462. Trefoil 7″ plate with plain center. Cambridge Glass Company offered this plate in other colors, both with and without a pattern of small blocks filling the center, in 1903. The black examples were probably made at Marion, Indiana, by Canton Glass Company in the latter half of the 1890's, and possibly by its successor from 1899, National Glass Company. Kemple Glass Works also made plates of this pattern, its #30 and #38 (catalogued as 7″ and 9½″ respectively) Open Edge Club plates, in the 1950's, but not in black. Other names for the design are Club and Shell* and Club and Fan Border*, and, with the figured center, Waffle Centre*.

463. Basketweave Base* plate, 8″, probably made by Fenton Art Glass Company from the same mold as Figure 93.

464. 8″ diameter Deep Pinwheel* plate, maker uncertain. A wholesale firm offered this in black and milk-white in 1898, as the Trilby* plate. There is some indication that this design had been reproduced by 1949. The name Trilby was used by United States Glass Company for another pattern, and is also the name of another item. Both the design shown here and others have been called simply Pinwheel*, and this one Pinwheel Border*.

465. Heart Border* 6″ plate, a design reportedly made by Canton Glass Company in the period 1893-1895. Black examples may date from a few years later, as Figure 462. Three sizes are said to have been made; the 8″ was reproduced (perhaps not in black) by Westmoreland Glass Company, as its #32, in the 1940's and later. This pattern has also been called Heart Shaped*, a name likely to cause confusion with other items.

466. Backward C 8″ plate, maker unknown, probably made between 1885 and 1905. See also Figure 458.

467. Two Chipperfield* cologne bottles, clear with black stoppers, possibly European, on unidentified 9″ tray, probably not the original for these bottles; likely period of bottles and tray, 1925-1940.

468. Atomizer, satin finished with gilt decoration, 7″ high, maker unknown, possibly 1920-1940.

469. Perfume bottle with owl face stopper, 5¼″, maker unknown, possibly European, probably after 1920.

470. Puff (?) box, clear with black cover, 3¼″ by 2½″ high, maker unknown, probably 1930's.

471. Paden City Glass Manufacturing Company's #215 Glades vanity set box, 1936. This pattern is also known as Sun Set* and Hotcha*.

472. Tray, 7½″ by 13″, with silver decoration. This appears to be the shape of tray which Paden City advertised in opaque white as part of a cocktail shaker set in 1932.

473. Dresser (?) box with metal cover, 8¾″ by 5″, maker unknown, probably 1925-1932.

474. Box and cover, 5¼″ by 5½″, reportedly to hold cosmetics for manicurists, maker unknown, probably 1925-1935.

475. Beauty box, probably lacking cover, 6″ by 6″, maker unknown, probably 1932.

476. Box, 5½″ diameter, probably for shaving accessories. This can also be found in milk-white and custard color, and an example is reported in a streaky opaque tan with a patent number which appears to be 1,892,310. This number dates from late 1932; the colors suggest McKee Glass Company as the maker.

477. Perfume bottle, 1¼″, made in France, date uncertain.

478. Snuff bottle, 2¼″, cameo glass, white outer layer carved in dragon design on black ground, probably Chinese, date undetermined, possibly as early as the eighteenth century.

479. Perfume bottle, 3¼″, with red cap and tassel, maker unknown, possibly 1920-1940.

480. Perfume bottle, 3″ by 4″ high, maker unknown, possibly 1920-1940.

481. Perfume bottle in shape of dog, with painted decoration, 3″, head removable, probably made in England about 1920-1935. On the bottom are the name and address Potter & Moore, London & Micham.

482. Tray, 2½″, for three triangular perfume bottles, maker unknown, probably 1920-1940.

483. Perfume bottle, 3½″, probably lacking stopper, possibly Czechoslovakian, probably 1920-1940.

484. 3¼″ gold-decorated bottle from Lanvin perfume, maker and date uncertain.

485, 486. Perfume bottles, 3″ and 4″, labeled in gilt "Nuit de Noel Can" (?), maker unknown, probably after 1920.

487. Vanity set, 4″, a puff box with a perfume bottle (stopper missing here) as the handle of the lid; painted decoration; maker unknown, probably 1920's.

488. Bowl with gold-encrusted etching featuring a horse-drawn coach; maker and decorator unknown, probably 1922-1940.

489. Candy box and cover, height 10¼″, with figure stem, maker unknown, probably 1925-1935.

490. Sandwich plate, like Figure 197 except for decoration. This one has Lotus Glass Company's Louise etching, gold-encrusted. Louise was probably made in the early 1930's.

491. An Imperial Glass Company or Corporation Molly* pattern piece, probably a muffin dish, 10½″, about 1930 or 1931, with unidentified silver deposit decoration. A larger Molly muffin dish was also made (perhaps not in black). See also Figures 169, 171, 172, and 431.

492. Perfume bottle with figure stem and metal fitting, 6″ tall, maker unknown, probably 1930's.

493. Cigarette box, 4¾″ by 3½″, probably Fostoria

Glass Company's #2391 large cigarette, about 1930, lacking cover, with unidentified silver deposit decoration.

494. Fostoria's #2373 small window vase and cover, 6¾" by 2" by 4" high, about 1930, with exceptional silver deposit decoration of unknown origin.

495. Puff box, 3½" by 3" high, probably made by The Akro Agate Company at some time in the period 1932-1951.

496. Three-toed puff box, 3½" by 3" high, maker unknown, probably 1930's.

497. Westmoreland Glass Company's #1701 trinket box. About 1980, this was made in black and hand painted with a white floral design. No other production of this shape in black is documented, though the mold had been in use many years earlier, probably around 1930.

498. A mismatch: Hazel-Atlas Glass Company's Colonial Block sugar cover (#13001 or 13001½), about 1929, on a 4" diameter puff box with patterned interior, maker unknown, probably 1925-1930.

499. Puff box lacking cover, 4½" by 2", maker unknown, probably 1930's. This has been reported in several other colors with two different glass lids, one with a figure of a sailboat, the other with a fanlike ornament.

500. Puff box lacking cover, 3¼" by 2" high, maker unknown, probably 1930's.

501. Deodorizer, 3" by 5" high, satin-finished, with metal cap; maker unknown, possibly 1920-1940. The bottom is lettered "BON AIR Made in USA".

502. Candy jar and cover, 5" by 5" high, maker unknown, probably 1924-1940.

503. Unidentified item, 8" across, possibly 1925-1935. Said to have been used as a change tray in hotels.

504. Daisy and Button* kettle ashtray, 2½" high, maker unknown, probably circa 1940.

505. Imperial Glass Corporation's #L4/1943 mug-type cigarette holder, 3¼" high, two-tone Black Suede glass, circa 1943. Original ad in *Glass Review*, May 1985, p. 16.

506. Pilot ashtray, made by Viking Glass Company after 1944, or possibly by its predecessor, New Martinsville Glass Company, 1937-1944.

507. Ash tray with dog figure, 4½" by 4¾", maker unknown, probably 1930's.

508. Ash tray in shape of coal scuttle, maker unknown, probably 1920-1940.

509A, B, C. Three electric cigar or cigarette lighters (some electrical fittings missing), respectively 2", 2½", and 3" in height, maker(s) unknown, possibly 1930-1935.

510. Ash tray, hat-shaped, 2½" high, embossed "DOBBS" on brim, maker unknown, probably 1920-1950.

511. Possibly a base for a gazing ball; compare Figure 551.

512A and B. Cigarette set (cigarette jar with match stand lid and three ashtrays), height 6" stacked as a unit, maker unknown, probably 1928-1935.

513 and 518. Two ash trays, maker(s) unknown, probably 1930's: (513) 3¼" by 2½" and (518) 3½" square.

514. Ash tray, fish-shaped, 3¾" by 4¾", maker unknown, probably after 1933.

515A and B. Set of four 2½" by 3" ash trays, maker unknown, probably 1930's.

516. Cigar or tobacco jar with animal-design wooden cover, height 6", maker unknown, probably 1915-1935.

517. 4" ash tray, maker unknown, possibly 1930's.

519. Match holder ash tray, 5" by 3" high, decorated with gold line; at least the match holder portion was probably made by The Akro Agate Company in the 1940's, as it appears to be the same as the jar in Figure 524.

520, 521, and 524. Three items made, reportedly by The Akro Agate Company, for Jean Vivaudou Co., a New York distributor of cosmetics. All have simple gold decoration. 524, the mortar and pestle, is a 3" jar and cover, circa 1944-1947. A label shows that this one originally held Orloff brand Bergamot shaving soap distributed by Vivaudou; others like it held men's deodorant. Jars like Figures 520 and 524 were also made in milk-white glass, to hold Orloff Attar of Petals products for women. 521, a 3½" mug marked with the Vivaudou firm's initials on the bottom, is said also to have contained Bergamot shaving soap. 520 when made in milk-white, 1943-circa 1947, was called an apothecary jar. Probably the black variety contained a product for men around the same time. It is 6" tall.

522. Beer bottle, 8½" tall, marked on base with Anchor Hocking Glass Corporation trademark and date (?) 1958, with metal closure. Company shows no records of ever having made black bottles. Some specialty items for company employees were made in small quantities and therefore not recorded.

523. This appears to be a combination cigarette server and ash tray made by Imperial Glass Corporation about 1943, yet this example, with a partial satin finish and gold decoration, is marked France on the base; diameter 4½".

525. Tumbler, 10-ounce, gold decorated, maker unknown, probably 1925-1935.

526. Marquette Watermark Detector, so marked on clear lid; maker unknown, possibly 1910-1935.

527. Pen holder, 3½" square, maker and date unknown.

528 and 529. Paperweights, respectively 4" in height and 3½" in diameter, #528 has original label: "Durant."

530A-D. Desk set with metal fittings, maker unknown, possibly 1930-1950: (A) rocker blotter, 4¾" by 1¾", (B) inkwell, 3¾" by 5¼", (C) paper clip holder, 3¾" by 1½", and (D) calendar, 4¾" by 2".

531. Paperweight, 2" by 2", maker unknown, probably after 1930.

532, 534, 536. Inkstands, maker(s) unknown, possibly 1925-1950: (532) base 4" by 4", (534) 3½" by 3¼" high, and (536) 4½″ by 3½″ high, marked "Property of U.S. Navy".

533. Inkstand, base 3″ by 4½″, labeled "Sengbusch", made for the Sengbusch Self-Closing Inkstand Company, of Milwaukee, Wisconsin, reportedly by the Union Stopper Company in 1917.

535. Rocker-type blotter with elephant figure, 3¼″ by 2¼″ high, made in several colors by L. J. Houze Convex Glass Company, beginning in 1931. The design was copyrighted in that year by Garrett Thew of Connecticut. The blotter was first made to Mr. Thew's order, but was later sold by Houze to various retailers, probably for several years.

537. Rocker blotter, with metal fittings, 5½″ by 2″, maker and date unknown.

538. Box with slot in cover, 1¾″ by 2″ high, no further information known.

539. Stamp rack, 5″ by 6″ tall; the wire loops are to hold rubber stamps. The metal cup at the top may be to hold a roll of postage stamps. The maker (possibly English) and date are unknown.

540-543. Electric lamps, makers unknown, each combining black glass with metal. Sizes and probable dates: (540) 13″ high, 1915-1930; (541) vanity stick, 6″ base, 1925-1940; (542) 12½″ high, 1930's; (543) a Hobnail* design, 8″ high, 1930-1935.

544. Sitting Bear* bottle, 10¾″ tall, maker unknown, reported to have held Russian kümmel (a liqueur) in the late 1800's.

545. Aladdin brand kerosene lamp, with clear font and metal connector and collars, 7″ by 8¼″ high, made by Aladdin Industries about 1937.

546. Electric lamp, Black Elephant* 3¾″ high base with amber globe which may or may not be original; maker unknown, probably 1925-1935.

547. Elephant, 7″ by 8½″ high, made by Gibson Glass, which advertised it in cobalt carnival in 1984.

548. Electric lamp, height 7″, maker unknown, probably 1930's.

549. Automobile headlight cover, 6″, marked Unity Mfg. Co., Chicago U.S.A. #9165. This was used during World War II blackouts.

550. Knife rest in shape of reclining dog, 5″ long, maker and date unknown.

551. Gazing ball of silvered glass on black base, 5″ high, maker unknown, probably after 1930.

552. Match holder, with painted flowers and metal frame, 3½″ long, in shape of a mortar (cannon), probably made about 1880-1910, possibly in Austria-Hungary.

553. Set of four 8″ stirrers with bowls in shapes of card suit emblems, each with a clear handle tipped with the color of the bowl: black spade and club, opaque red diamond and heart; maker unknown, probably after 1920.

554. Footed sherbet, 3″ high, with jade foot, probably made by Fenton Art Glass Company, circa 1931.

555. Four-ounce cocktail with opaque red bowl, probably made by the Pairpoint Corporation about 1920; the bowl color is said to have been called Flambo.

556. Figure of sitting dog, height 5″, maker and date unknown.

Items 557 through 566 are products of **Fenton Art Glass Company.**

557-559. Three vases in Fenton's Sophisticated Ladies decoration, date 1982: (557) #7561 vase; (558) #7655 sphere vase, 8½″; and (559) #7651 cylinder vase. See ad in *Glass Review*, Dec. 1982, p. 48.

560. #5177 Alley Cat (possibly Fenton's name for it), bought at the Fenton factory in 1969. This may have been a sample, as Fenton appears not to have put this item into regular production in black. The mold, reportedly designed by Reuben Haley, was first used by United States Glass Company to produce its #9448 Sassy Susie, probably introduced in 1924, which was made in black with satin finish and probably in milk-white. Fenton made this figure in other colors, embossed with a Fenton trademark, in 1970 and later. It has also been called Winking Cat* and Chessie Cat*.

561. 8½″ bud vase, mold number unknown, probably 1970's.

562. #5180 Wise Owl decision maker, lacking band, 4″ high, shown with top separated; reportedly this was made 1969-1972.

563. #5168 Owl, 3″, made in other colors 1980-1983, in black possibly in 1982.

564. FAGCA, *Reprints*, for 1962 (items list and one color page), 1963 (items list), 1964 (items list and one color page), 1965 (items list), and 1966 (items list); Fenton 1963 catalogue, p. 19, and July 1963 supplement, p. (2); Roserita Ziegler, "Researching With Roserita", *GR*, May 1982, p. 35, and June, 1982, p. 40; Linn, pl. 10; "Thumbprint", *Butterfly Net*, July 1985, p. 5.

565. Gail Krause, "Delightfully Duncan", *GR*, March, 1982, p. 11; Ferill J. Rice, "Happiness Is Fenton Glass", *Daze*, November 1, 1983, p. 10; Fenton catalogues, 1977-78 (pp. 1, 33, 40, 57, 63, 65, 67, 69, 72), 1979-1980 (pp. 28, 31, 35, 37, 38), and January 1980 supplement (pp. 10, 13); "From Fenton Glass Co.", *Daze*, May 1980, Section 1, p. 8; Fenton catalogues, June 1980 supplement (back cover), 1981-1982 (pp. 11, 23, 27, 29, 71), 1983-84 (pp. 4, 32), and January 1984 supplement (p. 2); James, p. 18; *Butterfly Net*, December 1978 ("Items to Be Discontinued", p. 8), January 1982 ("Items Discontinued From the Fenton Catalog as of January 1, 1982", p. 14). November 1982 ("Items Discontinued From the Fenton Catalog as of January 1, 1983", p. 14), and November 1984 ("Discontinued", p. 11).

566. Fenton 1963 catalogue, p. 19, and July, 1963 supplement, p. (2); Linn, pl. 9; "Thumbprint", *Butterfly Net*, July 1985, p. 6; "Gift Shop Display in 1968 Ebony Crest and Black Items", *Butterfly Net*, March 1983, p. 9; Ferill J. Rice, "Happiness Is Fenton Glass", *Daze*, October 1, 1986, p. 40; FAGCA, *Reprints*, items lists for 1963, 1964, 1965, and 1966; *LPG*, pp. 182-186 and pls. 15, 17, 18, 24, 59.

567A, B, C. Betty Newbound, "Along the Flea Market

so about 1949.

568-583, except 574, were made by **Westmoreland Glass Company.**

568. #1902 bud vase, bought new in the 1970's, possibly made in 1971. See also Figures 307 and 582.

569-571. Three #1049 Dolphin (sometimes called Shell Dolphin*) pieces: (569) candlestick, 9″, 1949-reportedly 1953 and possibly to 1955, (570) compote, 8″, reportedly 1953, and (571) candlestick, 4″, made in various colors as early as about the late 1920's and as late as 1979, date of black unproven. The dimensions given for these three items are per Westmoreland catalogues.

572. #1921 or Lotus pattern oval bowl, 11″, circa 1967. See also Figures 112, 316, and 575.

573. #1707 Huxford* napkin holder, 5½″, circa 1980.

574. Crystal Wedding pattern covered bowl or wedding bowl and cover, maker unknown, probably after 1944. This pattern was introduced about 1890 by Adams and Company of Pittsburgh, and continued from 1891 by Adams' successor, United States Glass Company, in clear glass, sometimes engraved, partly frosted, or color-stained. Reproductions began to appear in the 1940's, including shapes similar to this one. Since then, they have been made in various sizes and colors by Westmoreland (as #1874), United States Glass Company (as #712), and Jeannette Glass Company (as #3401 and #3412). While details vary among their products, none seems to match this one exactly. Adams' pattern name, Crystal Wedding, does not appear to have been used for these post-1940 pieces by the manufacturers, who did, however, adopt the new term "wedding bowl". Another, little-used, name for this pattern is Collins*. An unrelated pattern named Crystal Wedding was made by O'Hara Glass Company of Pittsburgh in 1876; it is advisable to name the manufacturer whenever possible in referring to these patterns.

575. #1921 or Lotus candle, 1967, shown here upside down as for possible use as a nut dish or the like, though this was not suggested by Westmoreland. See also Figures 112, 316, and 572.

576. #1900 slipper, 5″ x 2½″, with Westmoreland hand-painted decoration signed "C. McClais" (?), circa 1980. In 1981 this was offered in black with a different decoration.

577. #750 basket, 6½″, marked WG, circa 1971-1981. Several sizes were made (not necessarily in black) in the 1920's.

578. #5 Wren on Perch, 4″ high, marked WG, circa 1971 or 1980.

579. #4 Hen, marked WG, made in other colors circa 1949-1975 and 1980, exact date of black examples unknown.

580. #1881 Paneled Grape basket, oval, 7″ long, marked WG, made in other colors 1965-1981, exact date of black examples unknown.

581. #1881 Paneled Grape puff box/jelly or candy, height 4″, marked WG, made in other colors circa 1954-1981, exact date of black examples unknown.

582. #1902 small bell, crimped bottom, 5″ tall, circa 1981. See also Figures 307 and 568.

583. #75 Bull Dog, with brilliant (faceted clear glass) eyes, 2½″, marked WG, circa 1953 or circa 1971. Lancaster Glass Company's Toby Jr. and Fenton Art Glass Company's #307 novelty dog are very similar to this one; one which probably was made by Lancaster is recorded in black. The Westmoreland mold has been used since the Westmoreland factory closed.

Figures 584 through 598 were made for Tiara Exclusives, the home party merchandising plan operated by Lancaster Colony Corporation. 584, 585, and 586, which appear to be mold-blown, have been made by the Bartlett-Collins division; the remaining items were probably made by the Indiana Glass division of Lancaster Colony. These items are called here by the designations used by Tiara, as nearly as they can be determined.

584 and 585. Hobnail pitcher and tumbler, reportedly made in clear and other colors in 1975, 1978, and 1980, exact date of black unknown.

586. Regal water bottle, reportedly 1975.

587. Powder Horn tumbler, made in frosted clear reportedly in 1978-1982, exact date of black unknown.

588. Regal bowl, reportedly 1975; the deepest of three bowl shapes in this pattern.

589. Goblet, name if any and exact date unknown.

590. Probably the Hunters Horn mug reportedly made in clear glass in 1978-1982; exact date of black unknown.

591. Baluster zombie mug, reportedly 1973.

592. Art Deco tumbler, about 8-ounce, circa 1973-1974. This pattern was made in several other items in black at the same time; however, pieces in other colors had been made earlier, some reportedly around 1930, as Indiana Glass Company's #610. Other names for the pattern are Pyramid* and Rex*. See also Figure 397.

593. German drinking stein, 6″ per catalogues, made 1982-1987 and reportedly 1981. The same item was made, though apparently not in black, by Federal Glass Division of Federal Paper Board Company, Columbus, Ohio, until 1979.

594. Cameo ice tub and lid. About 16 items in this pattern have been made in black, this one and most of the others reportedly in 1978 only. The same pattern, chiefly in clear glass, is sold by Indiana Glass through retail stores as Diamond Point. It is important to name the maker when referring to this pattern, since either of its names could cause confusion with much older glass: Cameo is the name of a type of art glass, and of several older tableware patterns, none of which resembles this one; Diamond Point* is used for several other patterns which are similar to this one.

595. Mystique fruit or salad bowl, reportedly 1980.

596. Monarch butter and cover, reportedly 1975. This pattern was originally made many years earlier, in clear glass, as Indiana Glass Company's #123. It is also known by two other names: Panelled Daisies and Fine Cut* and Octagon Varient [sic]*.

Trail", *Daze*, April 1, 1983, p. 42 (567B decoration); Westmoreland catalogues, circa 1954 (p. 8, 567A, B, and C decorations), 1965 (pp. 8, 9, 567A, B, and C decorations), circa 1967 (p. 23, 567A, B, and C decorations), circa 1971 (p. 8, 567A and C decorations), 1977-78 (p. 29), 1979 (p. 28), 1980 (p. 18), 1981 (pp. 1, 23); Hammond 1, 1969 edition, pp. 129, 144 (567A, B, and C decorations), and 1979 edition, pp. 110, 120 (567A, B, and C decorations); Spillman, p. 356 (567C decoration); Belknap, pp. 20 (pl. 16a, possibly Westmoreland's), 271, 277, 289, 298; "Where Are the Molds?", *GR*, May, 1985, p. 33; Lafferty, *The Forties Revisited* 1, p. 61 (567B decoration), and *The Forties Revisited* 2, front cover; James, pp. 66-68; Millard, *Opaque Glass*, pls. 3, 8, 26; Brothers, p. 21; Cambridge Glass Company, *1903 Catalog*, p. 50; Ferson, p. 165; Lee *Fakes*, 1938 edition, pl. 65 and p. 151, and 1950 edition, pl. 93 and p. 185.

597. Honey dish and cover, reportedly 1973.

598. Colonial candy box and cover, 1984.

599, 600. Hens (covered dishes), each 7″ long, 6″ high, 599 all black, 600 black with white head, maker unknown; probably made for L. G. Wright Glass Company. This hen in other colors has been made at least as early as 1949 and as recently as 1981; the exact date of black examples is unknown. These are copies of an older dish, which is marked on the inside of the base with the name of its European manufacturer, Vallerysthal. A Hen and Nest which appears extremely similar was made in milk-white by Fostoria Glass Company, probably in the 1950's.

601. Dish with rabbit cover, 6″ long, 5½″ high, bearing Guernsey Glass Company mark, 1967 or later. The base is from a mold formerly used by The Akro Agate Company to make its #654 garden dish.

602. Westmoreland Glass Company's #26 Love Bird, a covered dish 6″ long, 5½″ high, bearing Westmoreland mark. This was made in other colors circa 1967-1982; the exact date of production in black is unknown.

603. Hen on Basket (covered dish) with white head, 6½″ long, made by Mosser Glass, Inc., in 1983 or later. This dish was introduced in 1983, but was not initially offered in black.

604. Bunny on a nest, a covered dish made by Boyd's Crystal Art Glass, Inc. In May, 1984, Boyd's advertised this and the items in Figures 606, 614, 619, and 621 as recently made in black (Ebony).

605. Mosser's #187 Duck on Basket with white head, a covered dish 5″ long and 4″ high. This carries Mosser's trademark, and was available in other colors in 1982 an 1983; examples colored as this one are probably more recent (compare comments on Figure 603).

606. Boyd's Chick salt, with Boyd trademark, made in 1984. The molds for this piece had been used first by Elizabeth Degenhart at the same factory, reportedly starting in 1966. Others have made very similar items in many colors, including Westmoreland Glass Company (its #3 Toy Chick) and the Vallerysthal factory in central Europe.

607. Boyd's Turkey covered dish, 5½″ long and 4½″ high, with Boyd trademark, probably made in 1984. The molds for this dish were among those first used by Degenharts, who reportedly began to make this dish in 1961. It is a reproduction of a dish made at the McKee factory in Jeannette, Pennsylvania, about 1900, and said to be usually marked McKee. It was also reproduced by the John E. Kemple Glass Works and probably by an unidentified factory, and a similar lid on a basketweave base has been on the market. The Crystal Art Glass factory, now operated by Boyds, is the only one known to have made any of these Turkeys in black.

608. Mosser's #173 Bird, 3″ long, 1½″ high, 1981-1986 in various colors, exact date of black unknown. Very similar figurines, with tails held higher, were Cambridge Glass Company's #3 (also numbered 13) Bird and one made by Westmoreland.

609. Viking Glass Company's #1311 Bird, made 1972-1984 and reportedly in the 1960's, exact date of black uncertain.

610-612. Three animals made by Imperial Glass Corporation from former A. H. Heisey and Company molds. Black examples of some animals from Heisey molds appear to have been feasibility test items only, while others were sold by the Heisey Collectors of America. (610) El Tauro (Bull), 7½″ long, 3¾″ high. Reportedly only about 30 of these were made in black, in 1983. (611) Tiger paperweight, 8″ long, 2½″ high, with Imperial's ALIG trademark, one of a reported 700 made about 1982. (612) Pig, 5″ long, 3″ high, marked ALIG, made about 1982.

613. Mosser's #177 Audubon Cardinal, made in colors 1981-1983, in black probably more recently (compare comments on Figure 603).

615. Mosser Owl, 4″, 1980's.

616. Swan, Big Pine Key Glass (FL), 4½″, Labeled, 1970's.

617. Horsehead, Maker unknown, Copy of Heisey stopper, 3½″, Marked with a B.

618. Degenhart Owl, 3½″, Marked, 1960's.

619. Boyd Debbie Duck and 3 ducklings, 2¾″ & 1¼″, Marked, 1984.

620. Satin Owl, Summit Art Glass Co., 3½″, Marked, 1980's.

621. Boyd Scotty, satin-finished, mini. of Cambridge book ends, 2½″ x 3¼″, 1984.

622. Bird, 2″, 1980's.

623. Rocky, Imperial Glass Corp. for Guerney Glass Co., Issue #5, Black Beauty, 4x3″, Marked, Made from Cambridge Glass Co. candy container mold, 1982.

624. Sammy, Boston Mould and Glass for Turner's Treasure Glass, the Rodeo Clown, 4¼″, Marked, 1981, The original issue was black and white marbled. Only 5 or 6 were all black.

625. Charlotte Doll, Unidentified manufacturer for Helen Rosso, 4½″, Marked, 1981, Copy of Royal Doultons figure 'Rose'.

626. Jenny Doll, Mosser Glass, Inc. for Vi Hunter Glass, 4″, 1981. Marked with Vi Hunter monogram.

627. Venus Rising, Imperial Glass Corp. for Mirror Images, Called Midnight Magic in black, 7″, 1981, Marked.

628. Sonny Boy, R. Wetzel Glass for Our Gang Collectables, 3½″, Marked; 1981, Never made in black for sale. This was a trial piece. Rare!

629. Standing Tall, Botson Mould and Glass, for J&B Glass Co., 5¾″, 1981, Marked.

630. Mosser Liberty Bell, 5¾″, Marked, 1980's.

631. Mosser #134 Bear, 3¾″, Marked, 1982.

632. Turtle, Botson Mould and Glass, for Helen Rosso, 5¼″ x 2″, Marked, 1980's.

633. Elephant, Maker unknown, 4½″ x 3½″.

634. Frog Toothpick, Unknown manufacturer for Helen Rosso, 3½″ x 2½″, 1980's. Copied from a much older toothpick holder.

635. Packy, a paperweight in the shape of a circus elephant. Botson Mould and Glass, for Craig Glass Art Collectibles, 3½″ x 2½″, Marked, 1980.

636. Clyde, Botson Mould and Glass, for Helen Rosso, 3″ x 3½″, Marked, 1981.

637. Train Engine, Unknown manufacturer for Helen Rosso, 4¼″ x 2¼″, Marked, 1982.

638. Drum Mug, Unknown manufacturer for Helen Rosso, 2¼″, Marked, 1982.

639. Mosser #194 Cat, 4″, Marked, 1980's.

640. Lucky, a figure of a unicorn, Boyd's Crystal Art Glass, 3½″ x 3″, Marked, 1984.

641. Boyd Kitten on Pillow, 3″, This item was made 1978-1982 only. The exact date of black is unknown.

642. Boyd Mini Pitcher, 2¼″, Marked, 1980's.

643. Boyd Toothpick holder, Baby shoe pattern, 2¾″ x 2″, Boyd mark, 1980's. Previously made in various colors by Degenharts; this was copied by them from a much older toothpick or match holder.

644. Mosser #193 Collie, 3″, Marked, 1980's.

645. Indian toothpick, Summit Art Glass, 2½″, Marked, 1980's.

646. Boyd Pooche, 3″, Marked, 1980's.

647. Salt dip, Squirrel pattern, Unknown manufacturer for Helen Rosso, 2¼″, 1980's.

648. Toothpick, Guernsey Glass Company, 2½″, Marked, 1980's.

649. Strawberry toothpick, Guernsey Glass, 2½″, Marked, 1980's.

650. Toothpick, Maker unknown, 2½″, 1980's.

651. Boyd Hand, 4½″, Marked, 1980's.

652. Teddy the Tug Boat, Boyd, 3″, Marked, 1984.

653. Bunny, Unknown manufacturer for Helen Rosso, 2″, 1980's.

654. Frosted Squirrel, 2″, 1980's. Reproduction of a former Cambridge Glass Co. novelty.

655. Frog, 1¾″, 1980's. Reproduction of a former Cambridge novelty.

656. Squirrel, 2″, 1980's. Repro. of Cambridge novelty.

657. Heart Salt Dip, 2″, 1980's.

658. Large Plate, Center inset, white enamel trim, 20½″. Possibly Czechoslovakian.

659. Ftd. Tray, Silver Rimmed Holder, English, 14″, Marked. On Silver: Made in England E.P.N.S., Yeoman Plate.

Ebony by Fenton

Classic shapes in jet black ebony. Perfect for any setting.

On order blank—page 3, column 1.

7521 BK
6" BOWL

7561 BK
10¾" VASE

7550 BK
6½" VASE

7557 BK
9½" VASE

7588 BK
TALL TEMPLE JAR

7488 BK
SMALL TEMPLE JAR

7558 BK
BUD VASE

7522 BK
IVY BALL

Black Glass from Fenton's 1981-1982 catalog pg. 50.

Crystal Satin and Black

For sheer beauty and elegance, Viking presents a select grouping of black and crystal satin pieces to mix and match together and with colors.

1431
10" Bowl

7733
7" Bowl

7841
Candle

1434
Compote

7730
Candy & Cover

7839
13" Bowl

1436
8½" Vase

1311
Bird

1311
Bird

1312
Candy & Cover

Pages 14, 15 from Fenton's 1978-79 catalog showing Black Glass.

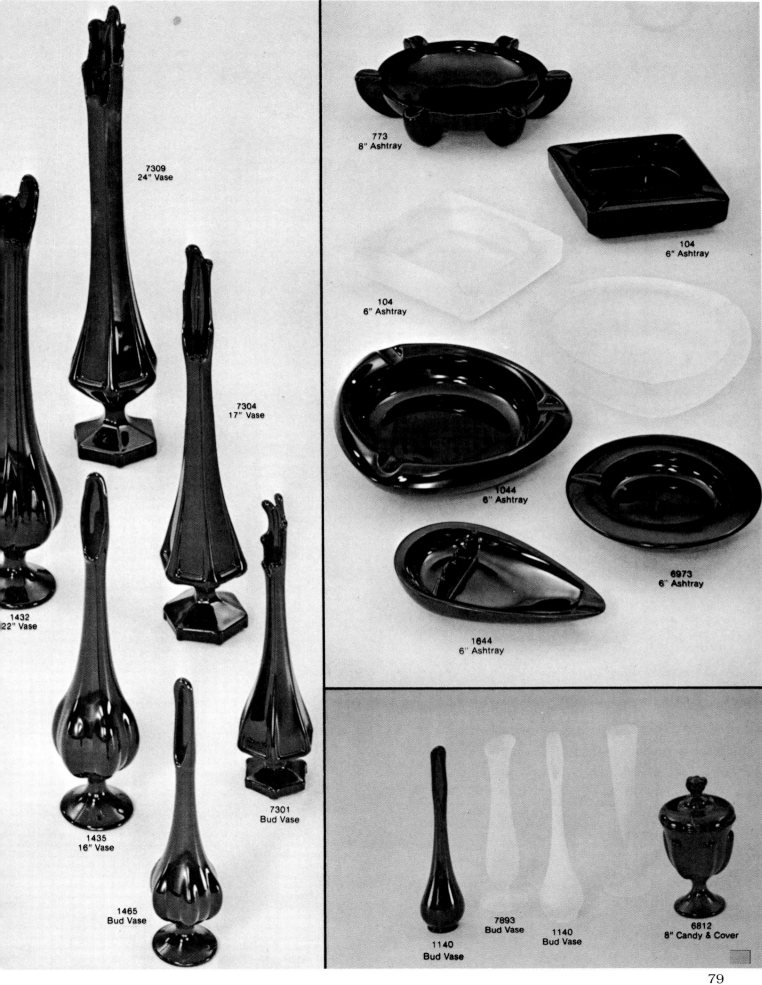

7309
24" Vase

7304
17" Vase

1432
22" Vase

1435
16" Vase

1465
Bud Vase

7301
Bud Vase

773
8" Ashtray

104
6" Ashtray

104
6" Ashtray

1044
6" Ashtray

6973
6" Ashtray

1644
6" Ashtray

1140
Bud Vase

7893
Bud Vase

1140
Bud Vase

6812
8" Candy & Cover

79

Black Glass

EXCELLENT SHAPES IN A HANDSOME COLOR— ESPECIALLY APPEALING TO THOSE WITH A FLAIR FOR THE MODERN TOUCH

229
Vase

3
Candlestick

3/12"
Bowl, Oval

3
Candlestick

1000
Cigarette Box

1000
Ash Tray

456
Ash Tray

1933
Candlestick

Black Glass from Westmoreland, shown from page 23 of the 1969 catalog.

5180 BK

5180 MI

Fenton page 47 – 1969 January catalog – Black Owl

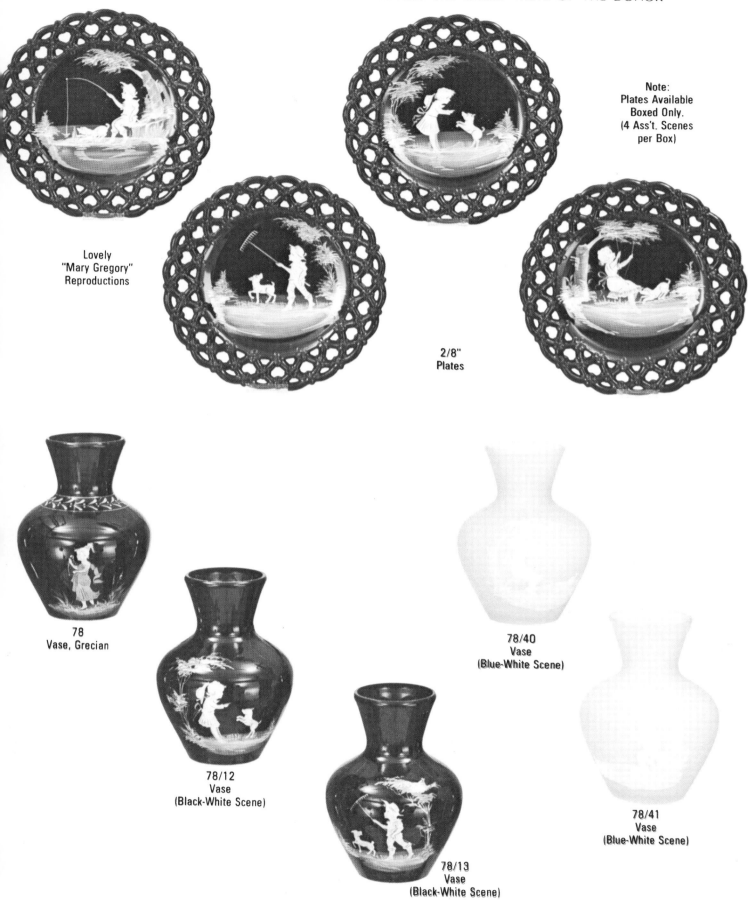

Note:
Plates Available
Boxed Only.
(4 Ass't. Scenes
per Box)

Lovely
"Mary Gregory"
Reproductions

2/8"
Plates

78
Vase, Grecian

78/12
Vase
(Black-White Scene)

78/13
Vase
(Black-White Scene)

78/40
Vase
(Blue-White Scene)

78/41
Vase
(Blue-White Scene)

Decorated Black Glass from 1969 Westmoreland catalog page 16.

Fenton Ebony in Thumbprint

4455 BK
Bud Vase

4438 BK
8½" Basket

4429 BK
Ftd. Comport

4453 BK
Tall Bud Vase

Plain & decorated Black Glass. Fenton 1975-76 page 28.

White Daisies

Delicately hand painted on striking Ebony glass, each piece is signed by the artist.

7380 WD
Ftd. Candy Box

4453 WD
Tall Bud Vase

4454 WD
8 Ftd. Vase

4455 WD
Bud Vase

Silver Poppies on Ebony

Beautifully handpainted and burnished silver. So very right for traditional, contemporary or oriental décor. Suggest to your customers that they polish just as they would their fine silver.

The glass with a very special class. By Fenton.

On order blank—page 3, column 1.

7550 PE
6½" VASE

7588 PE
TALL TEMPLE JAR

7521 PE
6" BOWL

7557 PE
9½" VASE

7561 PE
10¾" VASE

7488 PE
SMALL TEMPLE JAR

7558 PE
BUD VASE

7522 PE
IVY BALL

Fenton's 1981-82 catalog showing decorated Black Glass page 51.

Fenton
White Daisies

We've added several new lovelies to our daisy collection. These decorative and useful accent pieces really sell. Delicately hand painted on striking Ebony Glass, each piece is signed by the artist. Try it . . . you'll like it.

4455 WD
Bud Vase

4454 WD
8″ Ftd. Vase

5100 BK
Praying Boy and Girl

7380 WD
Ftd. Candy Box

5140 WD
Egg

4469 WD
Ash Tray

4453 WD
Tall Bud Vase

Two pages 30 and 31 from the 1973-74 Fenton catalog.

Fenton
Thumbprint Ebony

4438 BK
8½" Basket

4425 BK
Ftd. Comport

4453 BK
Tall Bud Vase

4454 BK
8" Ftd. Vase

4455 BK
Bud Vase

4429 BK
Ftd. Comport

85

Viking Black

For sheer beauty and elegance, Viking presents a select grouping of black pieces to mix and match together with colors.

7621
Cover

11" Cake Salver

1140
Bud Vas

1435
16" Vase

339 Large
Salad Bowl

7733
Individual
Salad Bowl

796
10½" Plate

707
14" Plate

8040
Glimmer

6827
6" Ashtray

1125
Lighter

790
8" Plate

7034
6" Ashtray

6625
4" Ashtray

7033
4" Ashtray

Viking Black Glass as shown in the 1980-81 catalog page 31.

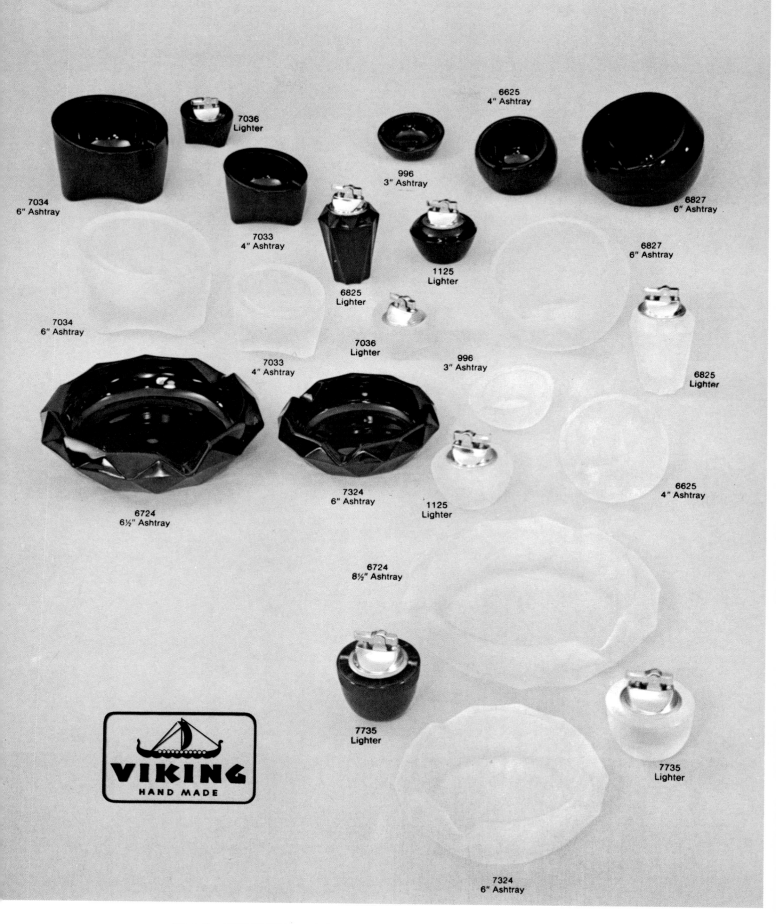

7036
Lighter

6625
4" Ashtray

7034
6" Ashtray

996
3" Ashtray

6827
6" Ashtray

7033
4" Ashtray

6827
6" Ashtray

1125
Lighter

6825
Lighter

7034
6" Ashtray

7033
4" Ashtray

7036
Lighter

996
3" Ashtray

6825
Lighter

7324
6" Ashtray

1125
Lighter

6625
4" Ashtray

6724
6½" Ashtray

6724
8½" Ashtray

7735
Lighter

7735
Lighter

VIKING
HAND MADE

7324
6" Ashtray

From the 1978-79 Viking catalog page 16. Black and Frosted smoking items.

Viking Black

For sheer beauty and elegance,
Viking presents a select grouping of
black pieces to mix and match
together with colors.

1140
Bud Vase

1435
16" Vase

6812
Candy & Cover

1432
22" Vase

6827
6" Ashtray

7034
6" Ashtray

7033
4" Ashtray

6625
4" Ashtray

1125
Lighter

Black Glass from Viking. 1979-80 catalog.

FENTON EBONY

Since the introduction in January of four pieces in Fenton Ebony the response has been so strong that we are offering a complete grouping of Ebony for your Christmas Season. Many of our representatives have spoken of the stunning displays Fenton dealers have created using Ebony and Milkglass.

4454 BK
Ftd. Vase

4455 BK
Bud Vase

4438 BK
8-1/2" Basket

4453 BK
Tall Bud Vase

4429 BK
Ftd. Comport

8252 BK
Empress Vase

9188 BK
2" Candy Jar

8251 BK
Mandarin Vase

3872 BK
Candle Bowl

4425 BK
Ftd. Comport, D. C.

4495 BK
Cigarette Lighter

4469 BK
6-1/2" Ash Tray

More shapes in Black Glass from Fenton. Found in July 1968 supplement.

89

Two pages from 1977-78 Viking catalog pages 12-13.

Ebony thumbprint from the 1969 Fenton general catalog page 13.

BIBLIOGRAPHY

BOOKS

Abbreviation	Author	Title and Publisher
	Allison, Grace	*Kemple Glass Works: 1945-1970.* Copyright 1977. Rainbow Review Glass Journal, Costa Mesa, CA.
	Anonymous	"Degenhart Update". Glass Review, Costa Mesa, California, no date (1978).
	Anonymous	*Glass Factory Year Book and Directory,* 1932 edition and 1937 edition. American Glass Review, Pittsburgh, Pa.
	Appleton, Budd	*Akro Agate.* Copyright 1972. No publisher or place stated.
Candlesticks	Archer, Margaret and Douglas	*Collector's Encyclopedia of Glass Candlesticks.* Copyright 1983. Collector Books, Paducah, Kentucky.
IG	Archer, Margaret and Douglas, coordinated and arranged by	*Imperial Glass.* Copyright 1978. Collector Books, Paducah, Kentucky.
	Avila, George C.	*Pairpoint Glass Story, The.* Special Edition. Arthur and The New Bedford Glass Society, New Bedford, Massachusetts, 1978.
	Barnett, Jerry	*Paden City The Color Company,* Copyright 1978. Privately printed.
	Batty, Bob H.	*Complete Guide to Pressed Glass, A.* Pelican Publishing Company, Inc., Gretna, Louisiana, 1978.
	Belknap, E. McCamly	*Milk Glass.* Copyright 1949. Crown Publishers, Inc., New York.
	Bennett, Harold and Judy	*Cambridge Glass Book, The.* Copyright 1970. Wallace-Homestead Book Co., Des Moines, Iowa.
	Bickenheuser, Fred	*Tiffin Glassmasters.* 3 volumes. Copyright 1979, 1981, 1985. Glassmaster Publications, Grove City, Ohio.
	Biser, Benjamin F.; chemically revised by J. A. Koch	*Elements of Glass and Glass Making.* Copyright 1899. Glass and Pottery Publishing Company, Pittsburgh, Pa.
	Blackwell Wielandy Company	*Glassware 1940,* "pages of Blackwell Wielandy Company's catalog of 1940-41." Copyright 1968. Antiques Research Publications, Mentone, Alabama.
	Bones, Frances	*Book of Duncan Glass, The.* Copyright 1973. Wallace-Homestead Book Co., Des Moines, Iowa.

	Bryce Brothers Company	*Reprint of a 1916 Catalogue of Lead Blown Glassware Manufactured by Bryce Brothers Company, Mount Pleasant, Pennsylvania.* Copyright 1984. The DAZE, Otisville, MI.
	Budget Publishing Company, The, compiler	*Directory of Glass Factories in the United States and Canada.* The Budget Publishing Company, Pittsburgh, Pa., 1937.
	Butler Brothers	*China & Glassware, 1925,* "pages of Butler Brothers' Midwinter catalog of 1925." Copyright 1968. Antiques Research Publications, Mentone, Alabama.
	Butler Brothers	*China & Glassware 1930,* "pages of Butler Brothers' Catalog of October, 1930." Copyright 1968. Antiques Reserach Publications, Mentone, Alabama.
CGC 1	Cambridge Glass Co., The	*Cambridge Glass Company, The, Cambridge, Ohio.* 1930-34 catalogue. Copyright 1976. Collector Books, Paducah, Kentucky.
	Cambridge Glass Company, The	*Catalogue of Table Glassware, Lamps, Barware and Novelties . . .* Cover title: *1903 Catalog of Pressed and Blown Glass Ware . . .* Copyright 1976. Harold and Judy Bennett, Cambridge, Ohio.
CGC 2	Cambridge Glass Company, The	*Fine Handmade Table Glassware by Cambridge,* 1949-1953 catalogue. Copyright 1978. Collector Books, Paducah, Kentucky.
	Corning Museum of Glass, The; Museum of Decorative Arts, Prague	*Czechoslovakian Glass 1350 1980.* Copyright 1981. The Corning Museum of Glass, Corning, New York; Dover Publications, Inc., New York.
	Covill, William E., Jr.	*Ink Bottles and Inkwells.* Copyright 1971. William S. Sullwold, Taunton, Massachusetts.
	Drepperd, Carl W.	*ABC's of Old Glass.* Copyright 1949. Doubleday & Company, Inc., Garden City, New York.
	Edwards, Bill	*Imperial Carnival Glass The Early Years.* Copyright 1980. Collector Books, Paducah, Kentucky.
Edwards, *Encyclopedia*	Edwards, Bill	*Standard Encyclopedia of Carnival Glass, The.* Copyright 1982. Collector Paducah, Kentucky.
	Emanuele, Concetta	*Stems.* Copyright 1970. Second printing, 1977. Wallace-Homestead Book Co., Des Moines, Iowa.

	Farrar, Estelle Sinclaire	*H. P. Sinclaire, Jr., Glassmaker*, volume 2. Copyright 1975. Farrar Books, Garden City, New York.
	Farrar, Estelle Sinclaire, and Spillman, Jane Shadel	*Complete Cut & Engraved Glass of Corning, The.* Copyright 1979. The Corning Museum of Glass and Crown Publishers, Inc., New York.
FAGCA, *Reprints*	Fenton Art Glass Company	*Fenton Selected Reprints 1952-1975.* Fenton Art Glass Collectors of America, Inc., no place or date stated (Appleton, Wisconsin, 1983).
	Ferson, Regis F., and Mary Fleming Ferson	*Yesterday's Milk Glass Today.* Copyright 1981. Authors, Pittsburgh, Pennsylvania.
	Florence, Gene	*Collector's Encyclopedia of Akro Agate Glass Ware, The.* Copyright 1975, "Values Updated 1982". Collector Books, Paducah, Kentucky.
FDG	Florence, Gene	*Collector's Encyclopedia of Depression Glass, The.* Sixth edition. Copyright 1984. Collector Books, Paducah, Kentucky.
EG	Florence, Gene	*Elegant Glassware of the Depression Era.* Copyright 1983. Collector Books, Paducah, Kentucky.
	Florence, Gene	*Degenhart Glass and Paper-weights.* Copyright 1982. Degenhart Paperweight and Glass Museum, Inc., Cambridge, Ohio.
	Florence, Gene	*Kitchen Glassware of the Depression years.* Copyright 1981. Also second edition, copyright 1983. Both editions, Collector books, Paducah, Kentucky. The 1983 edition is used except where indicated otherwise.
	Forsythe, Ruth A.	*Made In Czechoslovakia.* Copyright 1982. Author, Galena, Ohio.
	Gaddis, James H., O.D.	*Keys To Custard Glass Identification,* 6 booklets. "Keys 1" —"Keys 5", copyright 1971, 1974. Wallace-Homestead Book Co., Des Moines, Iowa; "Keys 6", copyright 1969. Early America Co., Pontiac, Illinois.
	Gardner, Paul V.	*Glass of Frederick Carder, The.* Copyright 1971. Third printing, December 1976. Crown Publishers, Inc., New York.
	Gillinder & Sons, Inc.	*Glassware,* Catalogue No. 25. Hillcrest Books, Spring City, Tenn., 1974.
	Godden, Geoffrey A.	*Antique Glass and China.* Copyright 1966. Castle Books, New York.

	Godden, Geoffrey A.	*Illustrated Encyclopedia of British Pottery and Porcelain, An.* Copyright 1965. Bonanza Books, New York.
	Heacock, William	*1000 Toothpick Holders A Collector's Guide.* Copyright 1977. Antique Publications, Marietta, Ohio.
H 2	Heacock, William	*Opalescent Glass From A to Z,* second edition. Encyclopedia of Victorian Colored Pattern Glass, Book II. Copyright 1977. Antique Publications, Marietta, Ohio.
	Heacock, William	*Rare & Unlisted Toothpick Holders.* Copyright 1980. No publisher or place stated. (Antique Publications, Marietta, Ohio.)
H 7	Heacock, William	*Ruby-Stained Glass From A to Z.* Encyclopedia of Victorian Colored Pattern Glass, Book 7. Copyright 1986. No publisher or place stated. (Antique Publications, Marietta, Ohio.)
H 3	Heacock, William	*Syrups, Sugar Shakers & Cruets From A to Z.* Copyright 1976. Antique Publications, Jonesville, Michigan.
H 5	Heacock, William, and Bickenheuser, Fred	*U.S. Glass From A to Z.* Encyclopedia of Victorian Colored Pattern Glass, Book 5. Copyright 1978. Antique Publications, Marietta, Ohio.
	Heacock, William, and Johnson, Patricia	*5,000 Open Salts A Collector's Guide.* Copyright 1982. Patricia Johnson, Marietta, Ohio.
	Innes, Lowell	*Pittsburgh Glass 1797-1891 A History and Guide for Collectors.* Houghton-Mifflin Company, Boston, 1976.
	James, Margaret	*Black Glass.* Copyright 1981. Collector Books, Paducah, Kentucky.
	Jarves, Deming	*Reminiscences of Glass Making,* second edition, enlarged. Beatrice C. Weinstock, Great Neck, New York, 1968.
K 1	Kamm, Minnie Watson	*Two Hundred Pattern Glass Pitchers,* fifth edition. Copyright 1939, . . . 1952. Motschall Company, Detroit, Michigan.
K 2	Kamm, Minnie Watson	*Second Two Hundred Pattern Glass Pitchers, A,* third edition. Copyright 1940, . . . 1950. Mrs. Oliver Kamm, Grosse Pointe, Michigan.
K 3	Kamm, Minnie Watson	*Third Two Hundred Pattern Glass Pitchers, A,* third edition. Kamm Publications, Detroit, Michigan. Second printing, 1956.

	Grover, Ray and Lee	*Art Glass Nouveau.* Fifth printing. Charles E. Tuttle Company, Rutland, Vermont, 1970.
	Hammond, Dorothy	*Confusing Collectibles,* 2 volumes. Volume 1, copyright 1969. Mid-America Book Company, Leon, Iowa; also revised edition, Wallace-Homestead Book Company, Des Moines, Iowa, 1979; volume 2, titled *More Confusing Collectibles,* copyright 1972. C. B. P. Publishing Company, Wichita, Kansas.
	Hand, Sherman	*Collectors Encyclopedia of Carnival Glass, The.* Copyright 1978. Collector Books, Paducah, Kentucky.
	Hartung, Marion T.	*First Book of Carnival Glass, Second Book of Carnival Glass, . . . ,* 10 volumes. Author, Emporia, Kansas. Book 1, second edition, 1968; Book 2, second edition, 1965; Books 3, 4, and 5, copyright 1975; Book 6, 1965; Book 7, copyright 1975; Book 8, 1968; Book 9, copyright 1970; Book 10, 1973.
CG	Heacock, William	*Collecting Glass,* 3 volumes. Copyright 1984, 1985, 1986. Antique Publications, Marietta, Ohio.
	Heacock, William	*Fenton Glass The First Fifty Years (A Pocket Price Guide).* Copyright 1984. No publisher or place stated. (Antique Publications, Marietta, Ohio.)
F 1	Heacock, William	*Fenton Glass The First Twenty-five Years 1907-1932.* Copyright 1978. O-Val Advertising Corp., Marietta, Ohio.
F 2	Heacock, William	*Fenton Glass The Second Twenty-five Years.* Copyright 1980. O-Val Advertising Corp., Marietta, Ohio.
H 4	Heacock, William	*Custard Glass from A to Z.* Encyclopedia of Victorian Colored Pattern Glass, Book 4. Copyright 1976. Antique Publications, Marietta, Ohio.
H 6	Heacock, William	*Oil Cruets From A to Z.* Encyclopedia of Victorian Colored Pattern Glass, Book 6. Copyright 1981. Antique Publications, Inc., Marietta, Ohio.
OPG	Heacock, William	*Old Pattern Glass According to Heacock.* Copyright 1981. No publisher or place stated. (Antique Publications, Marietta, Ohio.)

K 6	Kamm, Minnie Watson	*Sixth Pattern Glass Book, A,* second edition. Copyright 1949, 1954. V. R. Desmond, Grosse Pointe, MI. Fifth printing, 1970.
K 7	Kamm, Minnie Watson	*Seventh Pitcher Book, A.* Copyright 1953. Mrs. Oliver Kamm, Grosse Pointe, Michigan.
K 8	Kamm, Minnie Watson	*Eighth Pitcher Book, An.* Copyright 1954. Mrs. Oliver Kamm, Grosse Pointe, Michigan.
	Kimes, Arthur W. and Thos. A., compiled by	*Directory of Glass Factories in the United States and Canada.* Arthur W. Kimes and Thos. A. Kimes, Pittsburgh, Pa., 1929.
	Koch, Nora, editor	*Daze Past, The,* 2 volumes (volume 2 titled *The Daze Past 1976*). Nora Koch, Otisville, Michigan, 1976, 1977.
Krause, *Encyclopedia*	Krause, Gail	*Encyclopedia of Duncan Glass, The.* Copyright 1976. Exposition Press, Hicksville, New York.
Krause, *Years*	Krause, Gail	*Years of Duncan, The.* Copyright 1980. Heyworth Star, Heyworth, Illinois.
	Lafferty, James R., Sr.	*Fry Insights.* Copyright 1968. No publisher or place stated.
	Lafferty, James R., Sr.	*Forties Revisited, The,* volume 2. Copyright 1969. No publisher or place stated.
	Lafferty, James R., Sr.	*Pearl Art Glass Foval.* Copyright 1967. No publisher or place stated.
	Lagerberg, Ted and Vi, with descriptions by C. C. Manley	*British Glass.* Collectible Glass, Book 4. Copyright 1968. Modern Photographers, Ted and Vi Lagerberg, New Port Richey, Florida.
	Lattimore, Colin R.	*English 19th Century Press-Moulded Glass.* Barrie & Jenkins Ltd., London, 1979.
	Lechner, Mildred and Ralph	*World of Salt Shakers, The.* Copyright 1976. Collector Books, a division of Schroeder Publishing Co., Inc. Paducah, Ky.
Lee, *Fakes*	Lee, Ruth Webb	*Antique Fakes and Reproductions.* Copyright 1938. Author, Framingham Centre, Massachusetts; also enlarged and revised edition. Copyright 1950. Author, Northborough, Massachusetts.
LPG	Lee, Ruth Webb	*Early American Pressed Glass,* enlarged and revised, thirty-sixth edition. Copyright 1960. Lee Publications, Wellesley Hills, Massachusetts.
	Lee, Ruth Webb	*Sandwich Glass The History of the Boston and Sandwich Glass Company,* fourth edition, revised and enlarged. Copyright 1939, 1947. Author, Northborough, Massachusetts.

Lee, *Fakes Supplement*	Lee, Ruth Webb	*Supplementary Pamphlet No. 1 to Antique Fakes and Reproductions.* Copyright 1940. Author, Framingham Centre, Mass.
LVG	Lee, Ruth Webb	*Victorian Glass*, sixth edition. Copyright 1944. Author, Northboro, Massachusetts.
	Lehner, Lois	*Ohio Pottery and Glass Marks and Manufacturers.* Copyright 1978. Wallace-Homestead Book Co., Des Moines, Iowa.
	Linn, Alan	*Fenton Story of Glass Making, The.* Copyright 1969. No publisher or place stated.
	Lucas, Robert Irwin	*Tarentum Pattern Glass.* Copyright 1981. Author, Tarentum, Pennsylvania.
	Manley, Cyril	*Decorative Victorian Glass.* Van Nostrand Reinhold Company, New York, NY, 1981.
McCain, *Encyclopedia*	McCain, Mollie Helen	*Collector's Encyclopedia of Pattern Glass, The.* Copyright 1982. Collector Books, Paducah, Kentucky.
	McDonald, Ann Gilbert	*Evolution of the Night Lamp, The.* Copyright 1979. Wallace-Homestead Book Co., Des Moines, Iowa.
FPY	McGrain, Patrick, editor	*Fostoria — The Popular Years.* States "McGrain Publications . . . Frederick, Maryland", but published by Park Avenue Publications, Ltd., Racine, Wisconsin, 1983.
	McKearin, George S. and Helen	*American Glass.* Copyright 1941, 1948. Twenty-fourth printing. Crown Publishers, Inc., New York, 1975.
	McKearin, Helen, and Wilson, Kenneth M.	*American Bottles and Flasks and Their Ancestry.* Copyright 1978. Crown Publishers, Inc., New York.
	Measell, James, and Smith, Don E., with James Houdeshell, Aleda Mazza, Virginia Motter	*Findlay Glass: The Glass Tableware Manufacturers, 1886-1902.* Copyright 1986. Antique Publications, Marietta, Ohio.
	Millard, S. T.	*Goblets*, 2 volumes. Volume 1, copyright 1975. Wallace-Homestead Book Company, Des Moines, Iowa. Volume 2, copyright 1940. No publisher or place stated.
	Millard, S. T.	*Opaque Glass*, fourth edition. Copyright 1975. Wallace-Homestead Book Company, Des Moines, Iowa.
NM	Miller, Everett R. and Addie R.	*New Martinsville Glass Story, The*, 2 volumes. Richardson Publishing Co., Marietta, Ohio, 1972; Rymack Printing Co., Manchester, Michigan, 1975.

	M'Kee and Brothers, with introduction and text by Lowell Innes and Jane Shadel Spillman	*M'Kee Victorian Glass.* "Five Complete Glass Catalogs from 1859-60 to 1871". Copyright 1981. The Corning Museum of Glass, Corning, in association with Dover Publications, Inc., New York.
Morgantown	Morgantown Glass Works	*Old Morgantown Catalogues of Glassware.* Edited by Jerry Gallagher. Red Horse Inn, Plainview, Minnesota, no date (circa 1970).
	Munsey, Cecil	*Illustrated Guide to Collecting Bottles.* Copyright 1970. Hawthorn Books, Inc., New York.
CCG	National Cambridge Collectors, Inc.	*Colors in Cambridge Glass.* Collector Books, Paducah, Kentucky, 1984.
	National Cambridge Collectors, Inc.	*"Nearcut",* catalogue. Copyright 1985. The Cambridge Buffs, Study Group #7, Cambridge, Ohio.
	National Cambridge Collectors, Inc.,	*"'Near Cut' Value Guide No. NC-1".* Copyright 1983. The Cambridge Buffs, Study Group #7, Cambridge, Ohio.
	National Gift and Art Association, Inc.	*44th Semi-Annual New York Gift Show Hotel New Yorker and Hotel Statler February 23rd to 27th, 1953.* No publisher or date stated.
	Neal, L. W. and D. B.	*Pressed Glass Salt Dishes of the Lacy Period 1825-1850.* Copyright 1962. Authors, Philadephia, Pennsylvania.
	Newbound, Betty	*Figurine Facts and Figures.* Copyright 1982. Bill Newbound, Union Lake, Mich.
	Newton, Michele, and others	*Reflections Guernsey County Glass —1883-1987.* Degenhart Paper-weight and Glass Museum Inc., Cambridge, Ohio, no date.
H 5	Heacock, William, and Bickenheuser, Fred	*U.S. Glass From A to Z.* Encyclopedia of Victorian Colored Pattern Glass, Book 5. Copyright 1978. Antique Publications, Marietta, Ohio.
	Heacock, William, and Johnson, Patricia	*5,000 Open Salts A Collector's Guide.* Copyright 1982. Patricia Johnson, Marietta, Ohio.
	Innes, Lowell	*Pittsburgh Glass 1797-1891 A History and Guide for Collectors.* Houghton-Mifflin Company, Boston, 1976.
	James, Margaret	*Black Glass.* Copyright 1981. Collector Books, Paducah, Kentucky.
	Jarves, Deming	*Reminiscences of Glass Making,* second edition, enlarged. Beatrice C. Weinstock, Great Neck, New York, 1968.

K 1	Kamm, Minnie Watson	*Two Hundred Pattern Glass Pitchers*, fifth edition. Copyright 1939, . . . 1952. Motschall Company, Detroit, Michigan.
K 2	Kamm, Minnie Watson	*Second Two Hundred Pattern Glass Pitchers, A*, third edition. Copyright 1940, . . . 1950. Mrs. Oliver Kamm, Grosse Pointe, Michigan.
K 3	Kamm, Minnie Watson	*Third Two Hundred Pattern Glass Pitchers, A*, third edition. Kamm Publications, Detroit, Michigan. Second printing, 1956.
K 6	Kamm, Minnie Watson	*Sixth Pattern Glass Book, A*, second edition. Copyright 1949, 1954. V. R. Desmond, Grosse Pointe, MI. Fifth printing, 1970.
K 7	Kamm, Minnie Watson	*Seventh Pitcher Book, A*. Copyright 1953. Mrs. Oliver Kamm, Grosse Pointe, Michigan.
K 8	Kamm, Minnie Watson	*Eighth Pitcher Book, An*. Copyright 1954. Mrs. Oliver Kamm, Grosse Pointe, Michigan.
	Kimes, Arthur W. and Thos. A., compiled by	*Directory of Glass Factories in the United States and Canada*. Arthur W. Kimes and Thos. A. Kimes, Pittsburgh, Pa., 1929.
	Koch, Nora, editor	*Daze Past, The*. 2 volumes (volume 2 titled *The Daze Past 1976*). Nora Koch, Otisville, Michigan, 1976, 1977.
Krause, *Encyclopedia*	Krause, Gail	*Encyclopedia of Duncan Glass, The*. Copyright 1976. Exposition Press, Hicksville, New York.
Krause, *Years*	Krause, Gail	*Years of Duncan, The*. Copyright 1980. Heyworth Star, Heyworth, Illinois.
	Lafferty, James R., Sr.	*Fry Insights*. Copyright 1968. No publisher or place stated.
	Lafferty, James R., Sr.	*Forties Revisited, The*, volume 2. Copyright 1969. No publisher or place stated.
	Lafferty, James R., Sr.	*Pearl Art Glass Foval*. Copyright 1967. No publisher or place stated.
	Lagerberg, Ted and Vi, with descriptions by C. C. Manley	*British Glass*. Collectible Glass, Book 4. Copyright 1968. Modern Photographers, Ted and Vi Lagerberg, New Port Richey, Florida.
	Lattimore, Colin R.	*English 19th Century Press-Moulded Glass*. Barrie & Jenkins Ltd., London, 1979.
	Lechner, Mildred and Ralph	*World of Salt Shakers, The*. Copyright 1976. Collector Books, a division of Schroeder Publishing Co., Inc. Paducah, Ky.

Lee, *Fakes*	Lee, Ruth Webb	*Antique Fakes and Reproductions.* Copyright 1938. Author, Framingham Centre, Massachusetts; also enlarged and revised edition. Copyright 1950. Author, Northborough, Massachusetts.
LPG	Lee, Ruth Webb	*Early American Pressed Glass,* enlarged and revised, thirty-sixth edition. Copyright 1960. Lee Publications, Wellesley Hills, Massachusetts.
	Lee, Ruth Webb	*Sandwich Glass The History of the Boston and Sandwich Glass Company,* fourth edition, revised and enlarged. Copyright 1939, 1947. Author, Northborough, Massachusetts.
	Taylor, Dorothy	*Encore by Dorothy,* volume 1. Second printing, January 1984. Author, Kansas City, Missouri.
	Thatcher Glass Manufacturing Company, Salaried Personnel Department, compiled and edited by	*"Thatcher Glass Story, The".* No publisher, place or date stated. (Thatcher Glass Manufacturing Company, Elmira, New York, (1979?).
	Thuro, Catherine M. V.	*Oil Lamps The Kerosene Era in North America.* Copyright 1976. Fourth printing, 1981. Wallace-Homestead Book Co., Des Moines, Iowa.
	Thuro, Catherine M. V.	*Oil Lamps II Glass Kerosene Lamps.* Copyright 1983. Thorncliffe House, Inc., Toronto, ON; Collector Books, Paducah, KY; and Wallace-Homestead Book Co., Des Moines, IA.
	Toulouse, Julian Harrison	*Bottle Makers and Their Marks.* Copyright 1971. Thomas Nelson Inc., Camden, New Jersey.
	Umbraco, Kitty and Russell	*Iridescent Stretch Glass.* Copyright 1972. Cembura and Avery Publishers, no place stated.
	Unitt, Doris and Peter	*American and Canadian Goblets,* 2 volumes. Clock House, Peterborough, Ontario, Canada. Volume 1, 1971; volume 2, copyright 1974.
	Van Pelt, Mary	*Fantastic Figurines.* Author, Westminster, California, 1973.
	Van Rensselaer, Stephen	*Early American Bottles and Flasks,* revised edition. J. Edmund Edwards, Stratford, Conn., 1971.
	Walker, Mary	*More Reamers (200 Years).* Copyright 1983. Muski Publishers, Los Angeles, California.
	Walker, Mary	*Reamers (200 Years).* Copyright 1980. Muski Publishers, Los Angeles, California.

	Warman, Edwin G.	*Milk Glass Addenda.* Copyright 1952. Warman Publishing Co., Uniontown, Pa.
W	Weatherman, Hazel Marie	*Colored Glassware of the Depression Era,* 2 volumes. Author, Springfield, Missouri, 1970; Weatherman Glassbooks, Springfield, Missouri, 1974.
	Weatherman, Hazel Marie	*Decorated Tumbler, The.* Glassbooks, Inc., Springfield, Missouri, 1978.
WFG	Weatherman, Hazel Marie	*Fostoria Its First Fifty Years.* The Weathermans, Springfield, Missouri, 1972.
WPT 1	Weatherman, Hazel Marie	*1984 Supplement & Price Trends.* Glassbooks, Inc., Ozark, MO, 1984.
WPT 2	Weatherman, Hazel Marie	*Supplement and Price Trends for Colored Glassware of the Depression Era Book 2.* (Title varies.) Glassbooks, Springfield, Missouri, 1977; Glassbooks, Inc., Springfield, Missouri, 1979; Glassbooks, Inc., Ozark, Missouri, 1982. References are to the 1982 edition unless noted otherwise.
WFP	Weatherman, Hazel Marie	*3rd Fostoria Price Watch, The.* Weatherman Glassbooks, Ozark, Missouri, 1981.
	Welker, John and Elizabeth	*Pressed Glass in America.* Antique Acres Press, Ivyland, PA, 1985.
Welker, *Co.*	Welker, Mary, Lyle and Lynn	*Cambridge Glass Co. Cambridge, Ohio, The,* 2 volumes. Lyle L. Welker, New Concord, Ohio, 1970, 1974.
Welker, *Color 2*	Welker, Mary, Lyle and Lynn	*Cambridge, Ohio Glass in Color,* volume 2. Margaret Lane Antiques, New Concord, Ohio, 1973.
	Wetzel, Mary M.	*Candlewick The Jewel of Imperial.* Copyright 1981. Author, Notre Dame, Indiana.
	Wiggins, Berry	*Stretch in Color,* Book 1, Author, Orange, Virginia, 1971.
	Wilson, Kenneth M.	*New England Glass and Glassmaking.* Copyright 1972. Thomas Y. Crowell Company, New York.
	Zemel, Evelyn	*American Glass Animals, A to Z.* A to Z Productions, North Miami, Florida, 1978.

ORIGINAL TRADE CATALOGUES

BB

Butler Brothers

Our Drummer, May, 1906; August, 1906; Fall, 1906; June 1907; Mid-summer 1907; December, 1907.

Co-Operative Flint Glass Company, Beaver Falls, Pennsylvania

Catalogue, circa 1920. (Available in The Corning Museum of Glass, Corning, New York.)

Falker and Stern Company, "Direct Importers & Jobbers", Chicago, Ill.

Reliable Price List, Spring Catalogue, No. 18, April 15, 1898.

Fenton Art Glass Company, Williamstown, West Virginia

Catalog, January 1963; Catalog Supplement, July 1963; Catalog Supplement, July 1971; Catalog, 1977-78; Catalog, 1979-80; Catalog Supplement, June 1980; Catalog, 1981-1982; Catalog Supplement, January 1982; Catalog, 1983-84; January 1984 Supplement to the 1983-84 General Catalog.

Fostoria Glass Company, Moundsville, West Virginia

Fostoria The Crystal for America, copyright 1982, "Eastern Price List", January 1, 1982.

Imperial Glass Corporation, Bellaire, Ohio

Catalog No. 66A, no date (probably 1966); untitled catalogue, 1974-1975; *Handcrafted Imperial Glass*, 1975-1976.

Kemple, John E., Glass Works, East Palestine, Ohio

Undated price list (circa 1952); *Kemple Milk Glass Price List*, effective January 1, 1953.

Mosser Glass, Inc., Cambridge, Ohio

Master Catalogue, 1982; "Retail Price List January 1983".

United States Glass Company, The Duncan and Miller Division, Tiffin, Ohio

Hand-Made Duncan the loveliest Glassware in America, Catalog No. 93, no date (circa 1957).

Westmoreland Glass Company, Grapeville, Pennsylvania

"Westmoreland's Handmade, Hand Decorated Milk Glass, Crystal and Black Glass", no date (circa 1954); Catalog No. 75, no date (circa 1964); "Handmade Reproductions of choice pieces of American Glass", copyright 1965; untitled catalogues, no dates (circa 1967, 1971); 1972 Catalogue Supplement; 1974 Supplement; "Treasured Gifts", 1976 catalog supplement; *Westmoreland Hand Made Glass*, catalog 1977-1978; untitled brochure, no date (circa 1978); *"Gifts of Heritage"*, 1979 catalog; *"Gifts of Heritage"*, 1979 consumer catalog; *Gifts of Heritage*, 1980 Catalog; "The 1980 Collector's Series", folding brochure; *Today's Treasures-Tomorrow's Heirlooms*, 1981 catalog; *Today's Treasures Tomorrow's Heirlooms*, 1982 catalog.

PERIODICALS

	[Akro Agate Art Association newsletter]	Akro Agate Art Association, Salem, NH. Vol. 1, no. 1, June 1977.
	Akro Agate Gem, The	Akro Agate Art Association, Salem, NH. Nos. 1-15, June 1983 through First Quarter, 1985.
	Antique Trader Price Guide to Antiques and Collectors' Items, The	Babka Publishing Co., Dubuque, Iowa. Vol. 16, no. 5, issue 55, October, 1984.
	Antique Trader Weekly, The	Dubuque, Iowa, April 27, 1977, and Vol. 26, Issue 16, April 21, 1982.
AT Annual	*Antique Trader Weekly Annual of Articles on Antiques, The*	Dubuque, Iowa. Volume 3, no date (circa 1974).
	Butterfly Net	Fenton Art Glass Collectors of America Inc., Appleton, Wisconsin, and Williamstown, West Virginia.
CG&L	*China Glass & Tablewares* (earlier titled successively *China, Glass and Lamps* until 1942; *China and Glass* until before February, 1949; *China, Glass and Decorative Accessories*)	W. H. Barker; Commoner Publishing Co. Pittsburgh, Pennsylvania; Madison, N. J. Issues consulted include the May 1, 1957, *China Glass and Tablewares* Red Book Directory Issue.
C&GJ	*Crockery and Glass Journal*	New York, New York; East Stroudsburg, Pennsylvania.
Daze	*Daze, Inc., The* (titled *Depression Glass Daze* through December, 1981; *Depression Glass Daze, Inc.,* January 1, 1982-August 1, 1984).	Otisville, Michigan, Vol. 5, no. 12, February, 1976-Vol. 17, no. 5, July 1, 1987.
Facets	*Facets of Fostoria*	Fostoria Glass Society of America, Inc., Moundsville, West Virginia.
G&AB	*Gift and Art Buyer*	Andrew Geyer, Inc., New York, New York.
G&PW	*Glass and Pottery World*	Chicago. Various issues.
GC	*Glass Collector, The*	Peacock Publications. Columbus, Ohio; Marietta, Ohio. Nos. 1-6, Winter, 1982, through Spring-Summer, 1983.
GR	*Glass Review* (titled *Rainbow Review Glass Journal* until January, 1978)	Costa Mesa, California; Marietta, Ohio; Redlands, CA. Vol. 6, no. 10, October, 1976 through Vol. 17, no. 7, July, 1987.
	Harper's New Monthly Magazine	Harper and Brothers, New York. Vol. 64, December, 1881-May, 1882.
	National Duncan Glass Journal, The	National Duncan Glass Society, Washington, Pa. Vol. 7, no. 2, April-June 1982.
NGB	*National Glass Budget*	Pittsburgh, Pa.
	Paden City Party Line, The	Michael Krumme, Westminster, CA. Unnumbered, undated issue Vol. 2, no. 1, Winter, 1981).
P&GR	*Pottery and Glassware Reporter*	
	Spinning Wheel	Hanover, Penna. Vol. 23, No. 11, November, 1967.
	Western Collector, The	San Francisco, California. Vol. 9, no. 4, April 1971.

REFERENCES
By Figure Number

1. Stout, *McKee*, pp. 97, 103, 107; *W 2*, p. 267; *Daze*, February 1, 1979, p. 8.

2. Welker, *Co. 1*, p. 107, and *2*, p. 5; Bennett, p. 35; *CCG*, pp. 8, 9, 12, 13, 16-19; Mark Nye, "Cambridge Corner", *GR*, December, 1985, p. 15.

3. *CGC 1*, pl. 33-29B and p. 34-19; *W 2*, p. 42; Welker, *Co. 1*, p. 70; *CGC 2*, p. W5; Welker, *Color 2*, Pl. 6.

4. *W 2*, p. 50; *WPT 2*, p. 58; Ferson, pp. 106, 107; "What's New?", *GR*, Nov. 1984, p. 16; *Daze*, May 1, 1985, p. 30, and May 1, 1986, p. 41.

5. #214: *CGC 1*, pp. K, 31-18. #1070: Smith, *Cambridge*, pp. 54, 56; *CGC 1*, pp. 44, 45, 31-10, 31-13, 31-18, 31-27, 32-9, 32-22, 32-32, 33-21, 34-14; *W 2*, p. 40; *CGC 2*, pp. 31, 40; Welker, *Co. 2*, p. 11; *CCG*, pp. 66, 67.

6. *CGC 1*, pp. 32-35, 34-11; Julie Sferrazza, "Farber Brothers Facts", *Daze*, Nov. 1980, Section 1, p. 14; Phyllis Smith, "Cambridge Corner", *GR*, Sept. 1983, pp. 14, 16.

7. Smith, *Cambridge*, p. 21; *CGC 1*, p. 45; *CCG*, pp. 22, 23, 46, 47, 122, 123; *W 2*, p. 15; Bennett, p. 52.

8. *CGC 1*, pp. 33-7, 34-14, 34-16; Welker, *Co. 1*, p. 22; Welker, *Co. 2*, p. 18.

9. *CGC 1*, pp. 31-23, 33-23, and pl. 34-2; Welker, *Co. 1*, pp. 15, 16, 45; *Co. 2*, p. 64; Lafferty 2, p. 148; *CGC 2*, pp. 148-A, B, C, 152-D; *CCG*, pp. 118, 119; D. and J. McFadden and F. and V. Wollenhaupt, "The Cambridge Glass Company", *GR*, Jan., 1978, pp. 30-32, and Mar., 1978, p. 31; Bennett, pp. 31, 60, 61; Welker, *Color 2*, pl. 12.

10. *CGC 1*, pp. 33-20, 33-21, 33-23, 34-16; Welker, *Co. 2*, pp. 21, 22, 64; *CCG*, pp. 84-89, 116, 117.

11. A, B, C. *CGC 1*, pp. 31-10 through 31-13, 31-27, 31-28.

12 A-D. *CGC 2*, p. 243; Welker, *Co. 1*, p. 12; Bennett, p. 64.

13. *F 2*, pp. 39, 97; *WFG*, p. 166.

14. Smith, *Cambridge*, p. 46; *CGC 1*, pp. 46, 57, 62, 73, G, 31-10, 31-27, 31-29, 32-7, and pl. 34-5; Welker, *Co. 1*, pp. 22, 63, 89.

15. *W 2*, pp. 73, 125, 297; *NM 2*, p. 40; Smith, *Cambridge*, p. 32; *CGC 2*, p. 32-33.

16. Welker, *Co. 1*, pp. 93, 109; Mark Nye, "Cambridge Corner", *GR*, May, 1986, pp. 11-13.

18 and 19. *W 2*, p. 35; Smith, *Cambridge*, p. 52; *CGC 2*, pp. W3, W4; *CCG*, pp. 98, 99, 124, 125; Bennett, pp. 58, 59; Betty Bell, "More About Glass Swans", Koch 2, pp. Bell 27, 28; *CGC 1*, pl. 33-30; Welker, *Co. 1*, pp. 26, 52; *CGC 2*, pp. 36, 38, 46, 229; Betty Bell, "Identifying Your Glass Swan", Koch 1, p. 10; "Mosser Glass, Inc.", *Daze*, May 1, 1983, p. 48, and May 1, 1984, p. 57; Betty Newbound, "Along The Flea Market Trail", *Daze*, May 1, 1986, pp. 8, 9; *CGC 1*, p. 48; *CGC 2*, p. 23; *CCG*, pp. 124, 125.

20. *WPT 2*, p. 61; GC, Spring-Summer, 1983, p. 14.

21. Smith, *Cambridge*, pp. 7, 18, 44; Welker, *Co. 1*, pp. 38, 86; *W 2*, p. 38; *CGC 1*, pp. 15, 19, 53, 57, 58, 62, 68, 70, 71, 72, G, H, 32-9, 32-25; *Candlesticks*, pp. 39-41; Bennett, p. 65.

23. *CGC 1*, p. 33-7; Welker, *Co. 1*, p. 22; Welker, *Co. 2*, p. 11.

24. Smith, *Cambridge*, pp. 40, 41; *W 2*, pp. 39, 40; *CGC 2*, pp. 16, 31-2.

25. *WFG*, pp. 121, 159, 163, 194, 196, 216, 250, 259, 280, 281; James, p. 19; *Facets*, April, 1981, p. 5; *WFP* lists a few additional decorations, and lists the Pioneer items made in black.

26. Smith, *Cambridge*, pp. 54, 62; Welker, *Co. 2*, p. 94; *W 2*, p. 39; *CGC 1*, pp. 46, 32-32.

28. Smith, *Cambridge*, p. 54; *CGC 1*, pp. 46, 31-18; *CCG*, pp. 44, 45.

29. Smith, *Cambridge*, pp. 20, 60; *CGC 1*, pp. 45, 31-20, 32-32; Welker, *Co. 2*, pp. 21, 22.

30. Welker, *Co. 1*, pp. 51, 102; Smith, *Cambridge*, pp. 8, 57; *CGC 1*, pp. 32-4, 32-9, 34-11; *CCG*, pp. 12, 13, 40, 41, 60, 61, 70, 71; Bennett, p. 44.

32. *WFG*, p. 117.

33. "*Nearcut*", p. 95; Phyllis Smith, "Cambridge Corner", *GR*, July-August, 1983, p. 23.

34. *CGC 1*, pp. 31-14, 31-27, 32-22, 32-32, 33-7, pl. 33-30, and p. 33-B-11; Welker, *Co. 1*, pp. 22, 61, 84; *CGC 2*, pp. 67, 80, 128; *CCG*, pp. 92, 93.

35. *CCG*, pp. 20, 21, 40, 41, 114, 115; Bennett, pp. 17, 19, 22, 42; *H 4*, p. 59; *Candlesticks*, pp. 30, 31; Belknap, p. 110 and color plate; Gaddis, "Keys 5", pl. 6; Smith, *Cambridge*, p. 6; *CGC 1*, p. 33-11.

36. Smith, *Cambridge*, pp. 14, 46; Welker, *Co. 1*, p. 89; *CGC 1*, pp. 17, 47, 31-1, 31-5, 31-10; Welker, *Co. 2*, p. 13.

37A, B. Weatherman, "Sue Weatherman on Glassware", *Daze*, December 1, 1981, p. 31.

38. Batty, pp. 191, 193, 194.

39. *CGC 1*, pp. 41, 32-22, 33-7; Welker, *Co. 1*, p. 22.

40. Smith, *Cambridge*, pp. 45, 60; Welker, *Co. 1*, p. 67; *CGC 1*, pp. 42, 31-17, 31-27, 31-9; *CCG*, pp. 50, 51, 110, 111; James, p. 7.

41. *W 2*, p. 49; Bennett, p. 41, shows Co-Operative candlesticks in row 2 (misidentified). Similar design: Bickenheuser 2, pp. 65, 116, 135, 136; *W 2*, p. 337.

42. *CGC 2*, pp. 26, 208, 210, 223, 228; Welker, *Co. 1*, p. 17; *CCG*, pp. 14, 15, 92, 93, 108, 109; *Candlesticks*, pp. 21, 23; James, p. 7.

43. *CGC 2*, pp. 47, 78, 148-C, 152; Welker, *Co. 1*, pp. 16, 49; Welker, *Color 2*, pl. 10.

44. Welker, *Co. 1*, p. 100; Smith, *Cambridge*, p. 9; *CCG*, pp. 18, 19, 30, 31, 42, 43, 106, 107; Welker, *Color 2*, pl. 7; Bennett, p. 21; *H 4*, p. 55.

45. *CGC 1*, pp. 1, 53, 65, 66, 67, 68, 70, 31-32, 32-16, 32-21, 34-10; *Candlesticks*, pp. 18, 19, 33-36; Welker, *Co. 1*, pp. 19, 38, 52; Welker, *Co. 2*, p. 68; *CGC 2*, pp. 5, 26, 46, 79, 126, 141, 157, 162, 192, 195, 196, 199, 213; *CCG*, pp. 34, 35, 82, 83, 106, 107, 112, 1-13; Bennett, pp. 28, 30, 65; Welker, *Color 2*, pl. 6; Linda Whitaker in "Collector Close-Up!", *GR*, November, 1984, p. 15.

46. *WFP*, p. 136; *FPY*, pp. 68, 89. Introduction date is

based on comparison of pattern number with *WFG*, p. 240.

47. Smith, *Cambridge*, p. 43; Welker, *Co. 1*, p. 85; *CGC 1*, pp. 14, 19, 32-17.

48. *NM 2*, p. 15.

50. *CGC 1*, pp. 31-4, 32-16, 32-17, 32-20; *CGC 2*, pp. 19, 102, 109, 117, 123, 125, 200, 219, 231; Welker, *Co. 1*, p. 13; *Best of GR 3*, p. 27; Bennett, p. 54; Ruth Lombardo, "Black Glass A Personal Collection", *Daze*, March 1, 1980, p. 13.

51. *NM 2*, p. 57; James, p. 31.

52. Weatherman, "Sue Weatherman On Glassware", *Daze*, December 1, 1981, p. 29; Westmoreland catalogue, circa 1971, p. 22.

53. Phyllis Smith, "Cambridge Corner", *GR*, July-August, 1983, p. 25; Welker, *Co. 2*, p. 28; *CGC 2*, pp. 26, 58, 223, E2; *Candlesticks*, p. 26; Bennett, p. 65.

55. Fostoria bowl: *WFG*, pp. 171, 192, 193, 213, 215, 217, 250, 293.

58. *W 2*, pp. 315, 317, 377, 385; Butler Brothers, *China and Glassware 1930*, pp. unnumbered (16, 19); *W 1*, pp. 210, 211; Stout, *DG 2*, pl. 5.

59, 60. *W 2*, pp. 53, 392; *GC*, Spring-Summer, 1983, pp. 26-29; *CG 2*, pp. 47, 68; *WPT 2*, pp. 287, 293; *F 2*, p. 65.

61. James, p. 50.

62. *MH 3*, p. 109; *RP 3*, p. 26 and pl. 100; *H 6*, p. 9; *W 2*, p. 395; Edwards, *Encyclopedia*, pp. 220, 221; *WPT 2*, p. 288.

63. *MH 3*, p. 23; *RP 1*, p. 96 and pl. 215; *GC*, Winter, 1983, pp. 9, 46; *RP 4*, pp. 12, 10P; Hand, pp. 174, 175; Sophia Papapanu, "Depression From Carnival Molds", Koch 2, p. Papapanu 29; Edwards, *Encyclopedia*, pp. 132, 133; Edwards, *Imperial*, p. 63.

64. *MH 3*, p. 18; *GC*, Winter, 1983, p. 51; *RP 1*, p. 5 and pl. 12; Hand, pp. 176, 177; Edwards, *Imperial*, p. 11; James, p. 52; Edwards *Encyclopedia*, pp. 20, 21.

65. *W 2*, p. 53; *CG 1*, pp. 31, 32, 34; *F 2*, pp. 48, 49, 53, 57, 71, 72, 99, 103; Blackwell Wielandy Company, pp. unnumbered (16, 17); *GC*, Spring-Summer, 1983, p. 30.

66. *W 2*, p. 326.

67. *W 2*, p. 321.

68. *W 2*, p. 323; *F 1*, pp. 72, 88, 92, 93; *F 2*, pp. 66, 92, 93, 97.

70A, B. *W 2*, p. 326.

71. Betty Bell, "More About Glass Animals", Koch 2, p. Bell 23; Zemel, p. 261.

72. "From L. E. Smith . . . .", *Daze*, May 1, 1980, Section 1, p. 23; Van Pelt, p. 15; Mary Van Pelt, "Fantastic Figurines", *Best Of GR 3*, pp. 102, 103; Zemel, pp. 72, 215, 260; Newbound, p. 15; James, p. 33; *WFG*, p. 243; *FPY*, p. 89; *NM 1*, p. 46.

73. Betty Bell, "More About Glass Animals," Koch 2, p. Bell 23; James, p. 60; Zemel, p. 261.

74. *W 2*, p. 321; Zemel, p. 265; Betty Bell, "Identifying Your Glass Swan", Koch 1, p. Bell 10; James, p. 72.

75. "From L. E. Smith . . . .", *Daze*, May 1, 1980, Section 1, p. 23; Zemel, pp. 261, 262; James, p. 60; Edwards, *Encyclopedia*, pp. 116, 117.

76A, B, C. "From L. E. Smith . . . .", *Daze*, May 1, 1980, Section 1, p. 23; Zemel, p. 262; *Best Of GR 2*, p. 74; James, p. 33; Newbound, pp. 15, 16.

77. *W 2*, p. 326; James, p. 25; *W 1*, pp. 234, 235.

78. *W 2*, p. 326; Zemel, p. 82; James, p. 25.

79. *W 2*, p. 326; Zemel, p. 82; James, p. 25.

80. *W 2*, pp. 326, 164, 165; Barnett, p. 88; *CCG*, pp. 16, 17; *KG*, pp. 44, 45, 47.

81. *W 2*, pp. 319, 320.

82. *W 2*, p. 326.

83. *F 1*, pp. 67-69, 72, 92, 110, 111; *F 2*, pp. 28, 66, 140; Butler Brothers, *China & Glassware 1930*, p. (29); *MH 3*, pp. 113, 114; *RP 2*, p. 20 and pl. 74; *W 1*, pp. 216, 217; Wiggins, front cover and pp. 14, 15; James, p. 16; Ferill J. Rice, "Fenton Dolphins", *Daze*, March 1, 1984, p. 5; "New Finds", *Butterfly Net*, May, 1984, color page and p. 8; "Colors in Glass", *Butterfly Net*, March 1985, p. 6; Stout, *DG 2*, pl. 15 and *DPG*, p. 185; Fenton catalog supplements, June 1980, p. 5, and January 1982, pp. 5, 7; Roserita Ziegler, "Researching With", *GR*, September, 1980, pp. 24-26; "Items in the 'Fenton' Line To Be Discontinued—January 1, 1981", *Butterfly Net*, November 1980, p. 26; "Items Discontinued From the Fenton Catalog as of January 1, 1983", *Butterfly Net*, November 1982, p. 13.

84. *F 1*, pp. 68, 70, 110; Butler Brothers, *China & Glassware 1930*, p. (29); *F 2*, pp. 32, 34; James, p. 16; Ferill J. Rice, "Fenton's Lilac", *GR*, July-August, 1984, p. 28 and front cover; *Butterfly Net*, November 1984, color page; Ferill Jeane Rice, "Happiness Is . . . Fenton Glass", *Daze*, May 1, 1984, p. 7, and "Happiness Is Fenton Glass", *Daze*, September 1, 1985, p. 7 ("Colored Satin Etched Glass"), December 1, 1985, p. 40 ("More Concerning 'Etchings and Cuttings'"), and March 1, 1986, p. 39 ("Etched Vs: Engraved Glass"); Betty Newbound, "Along the Flea Market Trail", Koch 1, p. Newbound 27; Sophia Papapanu, "'Flash'", Koch 1, p. Papapanu 9; Zemel, p. 182.

85. *F 2*, pp. 26, 29, 64, 66, 68, 93; *W 2*, p. 107.

86A, B. *F 2*, pp. 5, 7-9, 29, 32, 34, 35, 50, 82, 130, 143, 149, 150; *W 2*, p. 103; FAGCA, *Reprints*, pp. unnumbered (items lists for July 1952-1957); Linn, pl. 1; Krause, *Encyclopedia*, pp. 32, 109; *W 2*, p. 140; *W 1*, pp. 224, 225; *CGC 1*, pp. 44, 33-B-8; Welker, *Co. 2*, pp. 11, 37, 64; *CGC 2*, pp. 40, 233; Welker, *Co. 1*, p. 15; *CCG*, pp. 22-25, 42, 43, 48, 49, 86, 87, 92, 93, 98, 99, 108, 109, 112-115; Barnett, pp. 24, 25, 82; *WPT 2*, pp. 209, 214; Koch 2, pp. Koch 23, 32; *NM 2*, pp. 10, 56; "Anchor Hocking", *Daze*, May 1, 1983, p. 65, and May 1, 1985, p. 34.

88. *GC*, Spring-Summer, 1983, pp. 32, 33, 35; *CG 1*, pp. 8, 9.

89. *F 2*, p. 86.

90. *F 1*, p. 111; *F 2*, p. 34; *GC*, Summer 1982, p. 12.

91. F 1, *pp. 67, 73, 110; GC*, Summer 1982, p. 12; *F 2*, pp. 28, 92; *GC*, Spring-Summer, 1983, pp. 28, 35.

92. *F 2*, p. 134; *F 1*, p. 110; *KG*, pp. 108, 109 (row 2, #2).

93. *F 1*, pp. 32, 52, 58, 74, 83, 104, 119; *GC*, Winter, 1983, p. 12; *RP* 1, pl. 12, A and B views; Kay Wahl, "Fenton's Basket Pattern", *Butterfly Net*, November 1984, pp. 4, 5; *F 2*, p. 28; James, p. 52; *MH* 1, p. 90; *MH* 8, p. 33; *H* 2, pp. 62, 82; "Black Carnival", *Butterfly Net*, March 1982, pp. 8, 9; Edwards, *Encyclopedia*, pp. 24, 25; Fenton Art Glass Co. advertisement, supplement to *Gift & Tableware Reporter*, first issue August, 1970; Fenton catalogues, 1977-78, pp. 37, 57, 61, 72, and 1979-80, pp. 28, 31, 36, and 1981-1982, pp. 20, 26, 28, and 1983-84, p. 2; Reichel 1, p. 10; Hammond 2, pl. 2; *Butterfly Net*, November 1983, p. 8.

94. *F 1*, p. 32; Kay Wahl, "Fenton's Basket Pattern", *Butterfly Net*, November 1984, pp. 4, 5; Ruth Lombardo, "Black Glass A Personal Collection", *Daze*, March 1980, Section 1, p. 13; James, p. 15.

95. *F 1*, pp. 17, 21, 44, 45, 71, 112; "Fenton's Ebony", *GC*, Winter, 1983, p. 12; *MH* 4, pp. 70, 71; *RP* 2, p. 14 and pl. 47; Hand, pp. 184, 185; *F 2*, p. 28; Edwards, *Encyclopedia*, pp. 132, 133; letter from Mrs. J. D. Blankenship, "Readers Say", *Daze*, April, 1979, p. 7.

96. *F 1*, pp. 69, 113; *W 2*, p. 104; FAGCA, *Reprints*, second page of "Items in the Fenton Line — 1941"; Betty Bell, "Those Gorgeous Glass Ladies", Koch 1, p. Bell 16 and "Fenton's Nude Lady", Koch 2, p. Bell 25; Betty Newbound, "Along the Flea Market Trail", Koch 2, p. Newbound 67; Roni Sionakides, "Fenton's Nymph", *GR*, May 1978, pp. 20-22; Betty Bell, "Etcetera", *Daze*, May 1, 1979, p. 3; "Answers from Mr. Frank Fenton", *Butterfly Net*, June 1980, p. 9; "Unknowns", *Butterfly Net*, May 1981, p. 12; Ferill J. Rice, "September Morn Nymph" (sic), *Butterfly Net*, January 1984, p. 11, and "Happiness is Fenton Glass"; "'Colors' with Fenton", *Daze*, June 1, 1984, p. 45, and "Fenton's 'Lilac'", *GR*, July-August, 1984, front cover and p. 28; *Butterfly Net*, March 1985, color page and p. 4.

97. *F 1*, p. 113; "Answers from Mr. Frank Fenton", *Butterfly Net*, June 1980, p. 9; *Candlesticks*, pp. 62, 63.

98. *F 1*, pp. 22, 44, 45, 47, 51, 53, 82-84; *K 7*, pl. 92; "'Persian Blue'—1917 Butler Brothers Catalog" and Ferill J. Rice, "'Persian Blue'— Fenton or Fenton Look— Alikes", *Butterfly Net*, May 1983, color page and p. 5; Ferill J. Rice, "Persian Blue—Fenton or Fenton Look Alikes", *Daze*, February 1, 1984, p. 7; *MH* 1, p. 40; "Ref: Colored Page", *Butterfly Net*, May 1986, p. 4; "Glass Collector Update" and "Collectors' Corner", *GC*, Spring-Summer, 1983, pp. 6, 45; Fenton Art Glass Company advertisement, supplement to *Gift and Tableware Reporter*, first issue August, 1970; Reichel 2, pp. 14, 17; Fenton catalogues, 1977-78, pp. 37, 58, 63, 64, and 1979-80, pp. 31, 34, 36; "Items the Fenton Art Glass Co. Will Be Discontinuing January 1, 1980", *Butterfly Net*, December 1979, p. 8; Fenton catalogue supplement, June 1980, p. 5; "Items in the 'Fenton' Line To Be Discontinued—January 1, 1981", *Butterfly Net*, November 1980, p. 26; Fenton catalogue, 1981-82, p. 40; "Items Discontinued From the Fenton Catalog as of January 1, 1983", *Butterfly Net*, November 1982, p. 14; Fenton catalog supplement, January 1984, p. 8; [Discontinued], *Butterfly Net*, November 1984, p. 10.

99. *F 2*, pp. 29, 31, 32, 38, 63, 81, 87, 92, 93, 97; Linn, pl. 1; Roserita Ziegler, "Diamond and Panel Design and 'Wisteria' Satin Etched Glassware", *Butterfly Net*, volume 2, #3, March 1979 (misdated March 1978), p. 5. Cambridge: Smith, *Cambridge*, pp. 9, 47; Welker, *Co. 1*, p. 90; *CGC 1*, pp. 52, 31-11, 32-5; James, p. 10. Imperial: *IG*, p. 209; *W 2*, p. 178. Paden City: Barnett, inside front cover, pp. 13, 59, inside and outside back cover; *W 2*, pp. 304-306; Betty Newbound, "Along the Flea Market Trail", Koch 1, p. Newbound 32; Jerry Barnett, "The Paden City Glass Manufacturing Company", *GR*, October, 1981, pp. 40, 41; James, p. 32; Uncertain manufacturer: Butler Brothers, *China & Glassware 1930*, p. (32).

100, 101. *F 1*, p. 109; *F 2*, pp. 34-36, 140; *W 2*, p. 396; William Heacock, "Fenton Convention Rarities Spotted", *GR*, October, 1980, p. 28, and *Butterfly Net*, November 1980, p. 10; James, p. 13; *Candlesticks*, pp. 62, 63; Reichel 2, p. 16; Gwen Shumpert, "Gwen's Glassline", *Best of GR* 3, p. 89.

102. *F 1*, pp. 65, 68, 69, 74, 92, 93, 111; *F 2*, pp. 40, 87; *MH* 3, pp. 113, 114; *RP* 2, p. 20 and pl. 74; *W 1*, pp. 198, 199; Ferill J. Rice, "Fenton Dolphins", *Daze*, March 1, 1984, p. 5; *Butterfly Net*, November 1984, color page; Stout, *DG* 3, pl. 6.

103. *F 1*, pp. 77, 97, 138 note 16; *F 2*, p. 60; Heacock, *Fenton Glass The First Fifty Years*, p. 103; Nora Koch, reported by, "Sanford Florida's 7th Annual Depression Glass Show and Sale", *Daze*, March 1, 1979, p. 7; *GC*, Fall 1982, p. 46.

104. *F 2*, p. 65; Ferill J. Rice, "Cover Story", *Butterfly Net*, September, 1982, pp. 1, 3, and "Fenton's 'Lilac'", *GR*, July/August, 1984, front cover and p. 28; Heacock, *Fenton Glass The First Fifty Years*, p. 103; "Recent Discoveries", *Butterfly Net*, September 1985, p. 10; *WPT* 2, pp. 290, 293.

105. *W 2*, p. 175; *IG*, pp. 156, 200, 201; *Daze*, October 1, 1986, p. 39; Virginia Scott, "Looking Through the Ads": "Imperial Milk Glass", Parts I and V, *GR*, February, 1986, p. 23, and June, 1986, pp. 12, 13; Imperial Catalog No. 66A, p. 15; Hammond, 1969 edition, p. 100; Reichel 1, p. 48.

106. *F 1*, p. 113.

107. *F 1*, p. 85; "Fenton's Ebony, *GC*, Winter, 1983, p. 12; "Recent Discoveries": "Were There More Pieces to the Rose Spray Pattern" and "'Blossom Spray'—Named by William Heacock", *Butterfly Net*, November 1983, pp. 7, 8; "Is It Fenton—or Is It Memorex?", *GC*, Summer 1982, p. 14; *MH* 5, p. 76.

108. *F 2*, pp. 29, 32, 96; *F 1*, p. 74.

109. *FPY*, p. 68; Virginia Scott, "Looking Through The Ads", *GR*, May 1977, p. 14.

111. Fostoria 1982 catalogue, p. 23, and price list, pp. 8, 19.

112. Westmoreland catalogue, circa 1971, pp. 21, 22, 23 (shows black), 24, 27; *W 2*, pp. 362, 278; Frances Bones, "Westmoreland", *Best of GR* 2, p. 12.

113. *FPY*, pp. 47, 69.

114. *WPG*, pp. 125, 182, 188; *WFP*, pp. 65, 73-75, 81, 83, 87, 88, 119.

115. *WFG*, pp. 113, 125, 183, 184, 186, 191, 210, 213, 214, 279; *Candlesticks*, pp. 70, 71; *W 2*, p. 243; *FPY*, pp. 193, 220, 232, 265; Ann Kerr, "Fostoria's Candle-Lights", *GR*, March, 1979, p. 33; Nora Koch, "Industry Update", *Daze*, December 1, 1981, p. 8; Fostoria 1982 catalogue, pp. 22, 23, and price list, p. 19; "Fostoria Glass Company", *Daze*, May 1, 1982, p. 46; *WFP*, pp. 62, 65, 73-76, 81, 83, 87, 88, 117-119, 122; James, p. 21; Stout, *DG 1*, pl. 7 (row III, #3), and *DG 3*, pl. 9 (row IV, #3); Edwards, *Encyclopedia*, pp. 200, 201.

116. *WFG*, pp. 120, 121, 161, 192, 216; *Facets*, April 1981, p. 6; *WFP*, pp. 63, 74, 76, 83, 84, 88, 89.

117. *WFG*, pp. 124, 168, 172, 195, 215, 219; *Facets*, December 1980, p. 7; Frances Bones, "Fostoria 'Fairfax'", *Daze*, April 1, 1978, p. 30; *WFP*, pp. 64, 77, 79-83, 88, 102, 103, 119; Ruth Lombardo, "Black Glass", *Daze*, November 1, 1984.

118. *WFG*, pp. 124, 253; *Facets*, December 1980, p. 6; *WFP*, pp. 64, 78, 79-81, 88, 102, 103, 105.

119. *WFG*, pp. 226, 235; *FPY*, p. 67.

120. *FPY*, p. 67; *WFG*, p. 112; *WFP*, p. 61.

121. Fostoria 1982 catalogue, pp. 6, 23, and price list, pp. 8, 19.

122. *WFG*, pp. 126, 171, 254; *WFP*, pp. 65, 78-81, 83, 88, 102, 103, 106; James, p. 21; *W 2*, p. 15; *Candlesticks*, pp. 74, 75.

123. *Facets*, March 1981, p. 5; *WFG*, pp. 225, 253, 256, 257, 259, 260, 294; *WFP*, pp. 90, 92, 104, 105, 107-110, 124.

124. *Facets*, March 1981, p. 4; *WFG*, pp. 225, 252, 253; Virginia Scott, "Looking Through The Ads", *GR*, March, 1977, pp. 14, 15, and May, 1977, p. 14; Glenita Stearns, "Glancing Back", *GR*, July, 1978, p. 10; *Facets*, October 1980, pp. 1, 5, 6; *WFP*, pp. 83, 89, 104, 105.

125. Cup: *WFG*, pp. 121, 157, 163, 194, 196, 197, 216, 259, 260, 269, 280, 281; *Facets*, April 1981, p. 5, and May/June 1983, p. 4; *FPY*, pp. 149, 191, 194, 231; *WFP*, pp. 64, 82-84, 88, 103, 109, 110, 113, 117, 118, 132. Saucer: *Facets*, March 1981, p. 4, and October 1980, pp. 5, 6; *WFG*, pp. 194, 225, 280, 281; *WFP*, pp. 82-84, 88, 89, 103-105, 118.

126A, B. *WFG*, pp. 121, 163, 213, 217, 259, 260, 288-290, 297, 298, 308; *Facets*, April 1981, p. 5, and May/June 1983, p. 4; *FPY*, pp. 149, 191, 231; *WFP*, pp. 64, 74-76, 87-89, 109, 110, 117, 122, 123, 125, 131.

127. *WFG*, pp. 113, 115; James, p. 19.

128. *WFG*, pp. 115, 117; Linda Whitaker in "Collector Close-Up!", *GR*, November, 1984, p. 15.

129. *WFG*, p. 126 and color page "Rose"; *FPY*, p. 67; James, p. 22.

130. *FPY*, p. 67.

131A, B. *W 2*, pp. 113, 126, 127; Stout, *DG 2*, pl. 22, row 3 (items 3 and 4 only); *W 1*, pp. 122, 123; Stout, *DPG*, pp. 118, 133, 134; *WPT 1*, p. 82; Richard Riegel, "You Say New Century, I Say Ovide", *Daze*, November 1985, p. 58; letter from G. K., "Readers Say", Koch 2, p. Readers Say 27; Batty, pp. 191, 192.

132. *W 2*, p. 126; *W 1*, pp. 88, 89; Stout, *DG 1*, pl. 3.

133. *KG*, 1981 edition, p. 127; *W 1*, pp. 58, 59; *W 2*, p. 114; Stout, *DG 1*, Pl. 11, and *DPG*, pp. 33, 34; Hazel Marie Weatherman, "'Picking Up The Pieces'", Koch 1, p. Weatherman 28.

134. *W 1*, pp. 58, 206, 207; *WPT 1*, p. 28; James, p. 71; see also Figs. 131A, B.

135A, B, C. *W 2*, p. 222; *KG*, 1981 edition, pp. 18, 19, 56, 57, 108, 109.

136. Spoon: "West Virginia Glass Specialty Company, Inc.", *Daze*, May 1, 1979, p. 8, and May 1, 1983, p. 45.

137. *W 2*, pp. 134, 140; *W 1*, pp. 44, 45; *WPT 1*, p. 19; Stout, *DPG*, p. 21.

138. Krause, *Encyclopedia*, p. 123; *KG*, 1981 edition, pp. 56, 57.

139. *W 2*, p. 124.

141 and 142. James, p. 25.

143. *W 1*, pp. 149, 218, 219; *WPT 1*, pp. 97, 98; Stout, *DG 1*, pl. 6, and *DPG*, p. 148.

144. *CGC 1*, p. 34-21.

146. Goblet in black: Ruth Lombardo, "Black Glass A Personal Collection", *Daze*, September 1980, Section 1, p. 3; Wetzel, pp. 32, 33; Virginia Scott, "Looking Through The Ads", *GR*, November, 1979, pp. 14, 15 and November, 1982, pp. 26, 27, and December, 1982, pp. 14, 15. Other information on goblet: Wetzel, pp. 15-17, 34, 40, 41, 43, 44, 58-61, 98, 99, and unnumbered page "Stemware", Scott, "Looking Through The Ads", *GR*, January, 1985, pp. 20, 21, and May 1983, pp. 12, 13; *EG*, p. 29; Koch 1, p. Readers Say 38; Imperial catalogues 66A, p. 24 and 1974-1975, p. 2, and 1975-1976, pp. 6, 7; Virginia Scott, "Glass Ad Search and Research", Koch 1, pp. Scott 8, 9, 24; "Steps in the Production of a Goblet", *GR*, March, 1978, pp. 22, 23; "Imperial—1980", *Daze*, May 1980, Section 1, p. 16; "Imperial Glass", *Daze*, May 1, 1982, p. 73; Scott, "Looking Through The Ads", *GR*, March 1983, pp. 6, 7.

147. Virginia Scott, "Looking Through The Ads", *GR*, May 1986, pp. 14, 15; Imperial catalogue 66A, p. 22; Hammond 1, 1969 edition, p. 119; Reichel 1, p. 31; Imperial catalogue 1975-1976, p. 36; "From Imperial Glass Corporation . . .", *Daze*, May 1, 1979, p. 9; "Imperial—1980", *Daze*, May 1980, Section 1, p. 17; "Imperial Glass by Lenox", *Daze*, May 1981, Section 1, p. 21.

148. *CG 3*, p. 5; Stout, *DG 3*, pl. 8 (bowl with optic); James, p. 29; *NM 2*, p. 58.

149. Hansetta Artware Company advertisement, "44th . . . New York Gift Show . . . 1953", p. 83; Frances Bones, "Not English Hobnail", *Daze*, July 1, 1977, p. 1 (picture includes 3-footed bowl attributed in *W 2*, pp. 320, 322).

150, 152, 153A, B. *IG*, pp. 122, 172, 173; *W 2*, p. 176; "Imperial Glass", *GR*, November, 1982, p. 34; Stout, *DG 3*, pl. 1 and p. 4; *China & Glassware 1930*, p. (29); James, p. 29; Edwards, Imperial, p. 60; Edwards, *Encyclopedia*, pp. 128, 129; *MH 1*, p. 35.

151. *W 2*, p. 169; William Heacock, "Catalogues Illustrated", *GR*, December, 1979, p. 43; *OPG*, p. 155; "Imperial Glass", *GR*, November 1982, p. 37; *China &*

Glassware 1930, p. (28); *K 1*, p. 99; Stout, *DG 2*, pl. 14, and *DPG*, pp. 102, 120.

154. Glenita Stearns, "Liberty's Square Luncheon Set", *Daze*, January 1, 1980, p. 1; *IG*, pp. 171, 185, 187, 189, 192, 195-197, 199; *W 2*, pp. 179, 287; *Morgantown*, p. 21.

155. *W 2*, p. 53; *WPT*, p. 61; *FDG*, pp. 200, 201.

156, 157. *W 2*, pp. 151, 161, 169; *W 1*, p. 67; Stout, *DG 1*, pl. 22; James, p. 28.

158. *W 2*, pp. 170, 351; "Imperial Glass", *GR*, November, 1982, p. 37; *China and Glassware 1930*, p. 28; Stout, *DPG*, pp. 14, 72.

160. Virginia Scott, "Looking Through the Ads", *GR*, August, 1986, pp. 10, 11; Imperial catalogue 66A, p. 8; Joan Cimini, "Imperial Glass", *GR*, May, 1985, p. 4; Hammond 1, 1969 edition, p. 113, and 1979 edition, p. 103. The mold number suggests that this design may have been made first in the mid-1930's.

161. Welker 1, pp. 19, 33; *CGC 2*, p. 289; Welker 2, p. 3; Joan Cimini, "Imperial Glass", *GR*, May, 1985, pp. 5, 6; *CCG*, pp. 14, 15; Bennett, pp. 56, 57; Welker, *Color* 2, pl. 6; Van Pelt, p. 14; Zemel, p. 12; "Where Are The Molds?", *GR*, May, 1985, p. 32.

162. "Imperial Glass by Lenox", *Daze*, May 1981, Section 1, p. 21; Milbra Long, "Cathay In Black", *Gr*, March, 1984, pp. 13, 15; Gwen Shumpert, "Gwen's Glassline", *GR*, December, 1986, pp. 13, 14; Van Pelt, pp. 30, 35.

163. William Heacock, "Unlisted Imperial Glass", *GC*, Summer, 1982, p. 39; "Question Box", *GR*, November, 1984, p. 30; Imperial catalogue 66A, pp. 1, 3; Hammond 1, 1969 edition, p. 112, and 1979 edition, p. 102.

164, 165. *W 2*, p. 396; James, p. 29.

166. James, p. 72; *F 1*, pp. 55, 109; *IG*, p. 204; *W 2*, p. 175; *Daze*, November 1, 1986, p. 1; Imperial catalogue 66A, p. 6; Reichel 1, p. 26; Hammond 2, p. 6; Joan Cimini, "Imperial Glass", *GR*, May, 1985, pp. 6, 7; Imperial catalogues, 1974-1975, pp. 30, 33, 36, and 1975-1976, pp. 27, 28, 30; "From U Readers", *GR*, November, 1976, pp. 40, 41; "Imperial — 1980", *Daze*, May 1980, Section 1, p. 17; "Imperial Glass by Lenox", *Daze*, May 1981, Section 1, p. 21; "Imperial Glass", *Daze*, May 1, 1982, p. 73; *CG 2*, p. 76; "Collector Report", *GC*, Winter, 1982, p. 19; *H 6*, p. 9; *OPG*, pp. 212, 216; "Collectors' Corner", *GC*, Spring, 1982, p. 42; Edwards, *Encyclopedia*, pp. 198, 199; *MH*, 3, p. 125; *RP 2*, p. 71 and pl. 267; *RP 3*, p. 51 and pl. 201; *W 1*, p. 192; *MH 5*, p. 138.

167. Joan Cimini, "Imperial Glass", *GR*, May, 1985, pp. 5, 6; Milbra Long, "Cathay In Black", *GR*, March, 1984, pp. 14, 15; Virginia Scott, "Looking Through The Ads", *GR*, June, 1980, pp. 16, 17; Van Pelt, pp. 29, 30, 34; Imperial catalogue 66A, p. 46; "Imperial Glass by Lenox", *Daze*, May 1981, Section 1, p. 21; Gwen Shumpert, "Gwen's Glassline", in Zemel, pp. 178, 179.

168. Virginia Scott, "Looking Through the Ads", *GR*, July 1980, pp. 26, 27; Van Pelt, pp. 31, 35; Mary Van Pelt, "Fantastic Figurines", *Best of GR* 3, pp. 52, 53; Gwen Shumpert, "Gwen's Glassline", in Zemel, pp. 178, 179.

169. *IG*, pp. 181, 185, 187, 195, 196, 199; *W 2*, pp. 171, 179.

170. *W 2*, pp. 151, 169; *FDG*, pp. 54, 55.

171. *W 2*, p. 287; *Morgantown*, p. 21; "Imperial Glass", *GR*, November, 1982, p. 33; *W 2*, pp. 171, 179; *IG*, p. 171.

172. *W 2*, p. 287; *Morgantown*, p. 21; "Imperial Glass", *GR*, November, 1982, p. 33; *W 2*, p. 179; *IG*, p. 171.

173. Shape: *WPT 2*, 1982 edition, pp. 203, 212, 228 (matching item), 229 (matching item), 235, and 1977 edition, p. 223; *W 2*, p. 247; Hazel Marie Weatherman, "'Picking up the Pieces'", Koch 1, pp. Weatherman 31, 32; *FDG*, pp. 140, 141; Barnett, pp. 52, 53. Etching: *W 2*, p. 305; *FDG*, pp. 148, 149; *EG*, pp. 108, 109; Betty Newbound, "Along the Flea Market Trail", Koch 1, p. Newbound 54; letter from "Ruth", "Readers Say", Koch 2, p. Readers Say 28.

174. Barnett, pp. 72, 80; Bickenheuser 2, pp. 113, 138, 145; Candlesticks, pp. 138, 139, 153, 154; James, p. 48.

175. *W 2*, p. 309; Barnett, p. 61; *KG*, pp. 124, 125, 179; Koch 1, p. DeLorme 5; Blackwell Wielandy Company, *Glassware 1940*, p. (6).

181-183. *W 2*, p. 318, *KG*, 1981 edition, pp. 24, 25, 70, 71, and 1983 edition, pp. 160, 162; Stout, *DG 2*, pl. 22.

184. *W 2*, p. 286.

185. Stout, *McKee*, pp. 103, 448.

186. *W 2*, p. 270; Stout, *McKee*, p. 102.

187. Stout, *McKee*, pp. 97, 102, 108; *WPT 2*, p. 182.

188. *KG*, 1981 edition, pp. 62, 63, and 1983 edition, pp. 124, 125.

190. Stout, *McKee*, pp. 190, 192, 193; *W 1*, pp. 232, 233; *KG*, 1983 edition, pp. 10, 11, 28, 29, 122, 123, 144, 145, and 1981 edition, jpp. 22, 23, 58, 59, 144, 145, 156, 157, 182, 185; Gaddis, "Keys 5", pl. 7; Rita DeLorme, "'Dutch Treats' in Depression Glass", Koch 2, p. DeLorme 12.

191. *W 2*, p. 270; Stout, *McKee*, p. 195; *KG*, 1981 edition, pp. 42, 43, 62, 63, and 1983 edition, pp. 124, 125.

192. *W 2*, p. 270; Walker, *Reamers*, pp. 66-68 and pls. II, III, and *More Reamers*, pp. 36, 82, 83; *KG*, pp. 64, 65, 126, 127, 144, 145, 188, 189; Stout, *McKee*, p. 22; *W 1*, pp. 194, 195; Hazel Marie Weatherman, "Hazel Marie Weatherman on Depression Glass", Koch 1, p. Weatherman 18; Gaddis, "Keys 4", pl. 8.

193. *W 2*, pp. 15, 271, 273; Stout, *McKee*, pp. 97, 98; letter from Marion Mirkin and reply from Ed Satchell, "Readers Say", October 1, 1979, p. 5; "From The Editor's Desk", p. 1, and "New Glass and China Issues To Beware Of", p. 40, *Daze*, July 1, 1979; letter from Anne Baughman, "Readers Say", *Daze*, September 1, 1979, p. 45; Sophia Papapanu, Koch 1, p. Papapanu 7.

194. Dithridge and Co. advertisement. *CG&L*, December 7, 1899, p. 5; Millard, *Opaque Glass*, pls. 34, 37.

195. Tray is shown in *BB*, May, 1906, pp. 128(?), 140, and August 1906, pp. 161, 177, and Fall, 1906, pp. 418, 419, 427, and June, 1907, pp. 196, 209, and Midsummer, 1907, pp. 91, 104, and December, 1907, p. 229. Other items in some of the same groups are

documented in Ferson, pp. 134 (Fig. 591, celery tray), and (Fig. 594, left).

196. Ferson. pp. 106, 109, 155; *BB*, June, 1907, p. 196, and Midsummer, 1907, p. 91, and December, 1907, p. 220; Florence, *Degenhart Glass and Paperweights*, pp. 23, 48, 49, 94, 95, 122; Tarter, front cover and pp. 5, 10, 11, 12; anon., "Degenhart Update", throughout; Barbara Sisson, "Bernard Boyd's Carmine", *GR*, December 1978, p. 16; Alma Collins, "'Boyd' Crystal Art Glass Update", *GR*, December, 1978, p. 33; anon., "Boyd's Crystal Art Glass Update", *GR*, January, 1979, p. 61; Boyd's Crystal Art Glass advertisements, *GR*, many issues in the period March 1979-February 1985.

197. *W 2*, pp. 234, 236-238, 241, 244, 245.

198. Viking Glass Co. advertisement, *C&GJ*, April, 1950, p. 17; *NM 2*, pp. 15, 57; Betty Bell, "Identifying Your Glass Swan" and "Glass Swans, Part III", Koch 1, pp. Bell 9, 13, 14, and "Swans and Animals Revisited", Part Two, *Daze*, March 1, 1978, p. 36; James, p. 72; Zemel, p. 227.

199. Viking Glass Co. advertisement, *C&GJ*, April, 1950, p. 17; James, p. 31 (which uses another item's pattern number for this one: compare *NM 2*, p. 15).

200-203B. *WPT 2*, p. 202; *W 2*, p. 384, bottom advertisement; Butler Brothers, *China & Glassware 1930*, pp. (29), (31); *CG 1*, pp. 67, 68; Stout, *DG 3*, pl. 13 (row II, #1, misidentified).

204. *NM 2*, p. 52; *W 2*, p. 298.

205. *NM 1*, p. 55; *W 2*, p. 299; *WPT 2*, p. 196.

206. Stout, *DG 1*, pl. 20; James, p. 51.

207. *W 2*, pp. 289, 397; Stout, *DG 3*, pl. 9 and p. 20; Uni and Keith Marbutt, "Jade-ite", *GR*, January, 1986, p. 13; James, p. 50; Stout, DG 1, pl. 20.

208. *NM 1*, p. 48; *W 2*, p. 298.

209. *W 2*, p. 291; *NM 1*, p. 43.

210. *W 2*, p. 320.

211. *W 2*, pp. 319, 320, 322; Koch 1, pp. Weatherman 6, 13.

212. *WPT 1*, 1973 edition, pp. 86, 87.

213. *W 2*, pp. 319, 320, 322; Koch 1, p. Weatherman 13; Stout, *DG 3*, pp. 20, 21.

214. *W 2*, p. 326; Koch 1, p. Weatherman 14.

215. *W 2*, pp. 321, 322; Koch 1, p. Weatherman 14.

216. *W 2*, pp. 321, 322, 325; Koch 1, p. Weatherman 14; Stout, *DG 1*, pl. 5; James, p. 35; Reichel 2, p. 71.

217. *W 2*, pp. 319-323, 325; James, p. 35; Koch 1, p. Weatherman 13.

218. *W 2*, p. 320

219. *W 2*, p. 326; James, p. 37.

220. Stout, *DG 1*, pl. 5

221. James, p. 40; Stout, *DG 1*, pl. 8; *W 2*, pp. 319, 323.

222. *W 2*, pp. 318, 320, 322; *CG 3*, p. 5; Weatherman, "Hazel Weatherman on Depression Glass", Koch 1, p. Weatherman 13; Stout, *DG 3*, pl. 4; James p. 38.

223. *W 2*. p. 318; James. p. 38.

224. *W 2*, p. 319; Stout, *DG 3*, pl. 8.

226. *W 2*, p. 323.

227. James, p. 38.

228. James, p. 38.

229. *W 2*, p. 318; Spillman, p. 346; James, p. 40.

230. *W 2*, p. 323.

231. *W 2*, p. 323; James, p. 39.

232. *W 2*, pp. 319, 320.

233. *W 2*, p. 318; James, p. 35.

234. *W 2*, pp. 321, 325; James, p. 36.

235A and B. *W 2*, pp. 15, 318.

236. James, p. 38; Stout, *DPG*, pp. 40, 114.

237. *W 2*, p. 318.

238. *W 1*, pp. 220, 221; *W 2*, pp. 318, 319, 323.

240. *W 2*, p. 319; James, p. 39.

241. *W 2*, p. 320 (matching items); James, p. 38.

242. *W 2*, p. 319; *W 1*, pp. 220, 221.

243. *W 2*, p. 319 (matching items).

245. *W 2*, p. 323.

247, 249. Frances Bones, "Not English Hobnail", *Daze*, July 1, 1977, p. 1 (reprints 1972 advertisement, which includes three-footed bowl shown in *W 2*, pp. 320, 322); Stout, *DG 3*, pp. 20, 21.

248A, B. See Figs. 131A, B.

250. *WPT 2*, 1982 edition, pp. 203, 212, 228 (#411), and 1977 edition, pp. 223, 241; *W 2*, p. 247 (#225 cheese only); Barnett, p. 48; James, p. 50.

251. *W 2*, pp. 319, 321, 322.

253. *KG*, 1983 edition, pp. 60, 61; Barnett, inside front cover and pp. 3, 44, 45, 58, 60; *W 2*, p. 397.

254. *W 2*, pp. 15, 318; James, p. 36; Stout, *DG 3*, pp. 28, 29; Peterson, *Glass Salt Shakers*, pp. 146, 172; *WPT 2*, p. 243.

255. *W 2*, p. 323; James, p. 36.

257. *W 2*, p. 319.

258. *W 2*, p. 323; *WPT 1*, 1973 edition, pp. 86, 87.

259. *W 2*, p. 320.

260. *W 2*, p. 325.

261. *W 2*, p. 323.

262. *W 2*, pp. 320, 325.

263. *W 2*, p. 320; James, p. 34.

264. *W 2*, pp. 321, 322; Weatherman, "Hazel Weatherman on Depression Glass", Koch 1, p. Weatherman 13; Belknap, p. 265.

266. *W 2*, pp. 320, 322; Weatherman, "Hazel Weatherman on Depression Glass", Koch 1, p. Weatherman 13; James, p. 34.

267. *W 2*, p. 326; *W 1*, pp. 200, 201; Stout, *DG 3*, pp. 22, 23; *WPT 1*, p. 134.

268. *W 2*, p. 321.

269. Stout, *DG 3*, pp. 22, 23; *W 2*, pp. 321, 322, 325.

270. *W* 2, pp. 321, 322, 325.

271. Bickenheuser 2, pp. 70, 113, 133, 149; Margaret Laneve, "Black Satin Glass", *AT Annual* 3, p. 181.

272. Bickenheuser 2, pp. 134, 140; Stout, *DG* 3, pp. 24, 25, 34, 35; *W* 2, p. 348.

273. Bickenheuser 2, front cover and pp. 70, 95, 113, 132, 145; *CCG*, pp. 20-23, 106, 107; Welker, *Color* 2, pl. 5; Bennett, p. 22; *Candlesticks*, pp. 24, 25, 152, 153; Margaret Laneve, "Black Satin Glass", *AT Annual* 3, p. 180.

274. Lafferty, *Fry Insights*, reprint of Catalogue No. 10, p. 18; Lafferty, *Pearl Art Glass Foval*, reprint of "Fry's Art Glass", p. 16; *Daze*, June 1, 1987, p. 1; Welker, *Co. 1*, pp. 97, 104; Smith, *Cambridge*, p. 7; *CGC 1*, pp. 12, 13, 18, 19; Bennett, pp. 66, 74; Welker, *Color* 2, pl. 7; *W* 2, pp. 25, 332, 335; Butler Brothers, *China and Glassware 1925*, p. (12), and *China and Glassware 1930*, p. (32).

275. Bickenheuser 2, pp. 65, 95, 135, 149; Fred Bickenheuser, "Tiffin Glassmasters", *GR*, January-February, 1982, p. 3; Bettye Waher, "Show and Tell", *GR*, April, 1981, pp. 16, 17; Margaret Laneve, "Black Satin Glass", *AT Annual* 3, p. 180.

276. Bowl: Bickenheuser 2, pp. 116, 132; *W* 2, p. 339; Wiggins, pp. 22, 23; Stout, *DG* 3, pp. 34, 35. Base: Bickenheuser 2, pp. 65, 74, 116, 134; *W* 2, p. 339; Albert Christian Revi, "Black Satin Glassware", *SW Antiques*, p. 371; Butler Brothers, *China and Glassware 1925*, p. (11); *Berry Wiggins*, "Black Bases", *Butterfly Net*, January 1984, pp. 3, 4; Margaret Laneve, "Black Satin Glass", *AT Annual* 3, p. 180. Westmoreland: "Westmoreland's Handmade . . . Glass", circa 1954 brochure, pp. 3, 8; *Candlesticks*, p. 172; Westmoreland catalogue, circa 1971, p. 1.

277. Bickenheuser 2, p. 133; Belknap, p. 44; *Candlesticks*, pp. 156, 157, 161, 162, 164, 165; *CG* 1, pp. 60, 61, 63; *H* 5, pp. 13, 22, 157.

278. Bickenheuser 2, pp. 95, 142, 149; *WPT 2*, p. 257; Fred Bickenheuser, "Tiffin Glassmasters", *GR*, January-February 1982, p. 3; Margaret Laneve, "Black Satin Glass", *AT Annual* 3, p. 180.

279. Bickenheuser 2, p. 140.

280. Bickenheuser 2, pp. 116, 133; *W* 2, p. 340; Mary Van Pelt, "Fantastic Figurines", *GR*, August, 1977, pp. 22, 23.

281. *WPT 2*, p. 257. Matching items: Bickenheuser 3, p. 178; Bickenheuser 2, p. 138.

282. *Bickenheuser 2, pp. 30, 59, 80, 115, 117, 127, 131, 136, 137, 139, 143*; *W* 2, p. 340; "Gift Goods", *GR*, August, 1980, p. 40.

283. *W* 2, p. 345; Bickenheuser 1, p. 102; *W* 1, pp. 218, 219; Margaret Laneve, "Black Satin Glass", *AT Annual* 3, p. 180; *CG* 1, pp. 57, 101; James, p. 44.

284. *WPT 1*, 1973 edition, pp. 76, 77; Sandra McPhee Stout, "That Sparkling Dinnerware and Related Items from the Depression", *The Western Collector*, April 1971, p. 12B; Roni Sionakides, ed., "Question Box", *GR*, July, 1980, p. 43.

285. *W* 2, pp. 346, 347; *W* 1, pp. 196, 197; James, p. 42.

286. Bickenheuser 2, pp. 115, 138.

288. Albert Christian Revi, "Black Satin Glassware", *SW Antiques*, p. 371; Bickenheuser 2, pp. 61, 116, 117, 131, 132, 137; Bickenheuser 1, pp. 66, 76; *W* 2, p. 343; Margaret Laneve, "Black Satin Glass", *AT Annual* 3, p. 181; Smith, *Cambridge*, p. 7; *CGC1*, p. 53; *CCG*, pp. 22, 23; *F 2*, p. 93; *W* 2, pp. 23, 28; *Candlesticks*, pp. 152, 153.

289. Bickenheuser 3, pp. 56, 59, 63, 105-115, 184.

290. Shape: Bickenheuser 2, pp. 12, 30, 33, 65, 68, 70, 77, 78, 114, 117, 119, 130, 131, 137; Bickenheuser 2, p. 115.

291. *W* 2, p. 345; Bickenheuser 1, front cover and p. 102; "Artware, Giftware and Tableware of Enduring Charm", *GR*, August, 1976, p. 43; Margaret Laneve, "Black Satin Glass", *AT Annual* 3, pp. 180, 181; Bickenheuser 3, p. 62.

292. Bickenheuser 1, p. 102; Margaret Laneve, "Black Satin Glass", *AT Annual* 3, p. 181; James, p. 41.

293. Bickenheuser 2, pp. 61, 132.

294. Lafferty, *Fry Insights*, front cover and Catalogue No. 10 reprint, p. 18; *Daze*, June 1, 1987, p. 1.

295, 296. *W*, p. 348; *W* 1, pp. 204, 205.

299, 300A. B. *W* 1, pp. 212, 213, 218, 219; Stout, *DG* 2, pl. 22; *W* 2, p. 347.

301. *W* 2, p. 290; *NM* 2, p. 49; *NM* 1, p. 44; *GC* 6, pp. 31, 37.

303. *F 1*, pp. 89, 90; Umbraco, pp. 28, 29.

305. Hansetta Artware Company advertisement in "44th . . . New York Gift Show . . . 1953", p. 83.

306. Stout, *DG* 2, pl. 24; "Readers Say", *Daze*, January, 1981, p. 27; *W* 2, p. 378.

307. Westmoreland catalogues: circa 1971, pp. 3, 17, and 1974 supplement, p. 4, and 1976 supplement, p. 1, and 1977-78, pp. 1, 3-5, 11, and circa 1978 brochure, pp. 1, 3, 6, and 1979, pp. 25, 34, 36, 37, and 1979 consumer catalog, pp. 25, 34, 36, 37; *W* 2, pp. 361, 379.

308. Iris and Joe Caleb in various authors, "Powder Jars", *Daze*, March 1, 1978, p. 32; *CG* 3, pp. 38, 50.

310. Belknap, pp. 154, 273, 274, 299; Westmoreland advertisement, *CG&L*, February, 1949, p. 1; Koch 1, p. Catalog Reprint 6; Nora Koch, "Glassroots Research", Koch 2, p. Koch 34; Millard, *Opaque Glass*, pl. 285; Westmoreland catalogues, circa 1954 (p. 2), circa 1964 (pp. 2, 4, 6, 8), circa 1967 (p. 12), 1971 (p. 6), 1974 supplement (p. 9), 1976 supplement (p. 8), 1980 (p. 35), 1980 folder, 1981 (p. 39); Hammond 1, 1969 edition, p. 145, and 1979 edition, p. 121; "From Westmoreland Glass Company", *Daze*, May 1980, pp. 20, 21; Ferson, p. 164; Lee, *Fakes*, 1950 edition, p. 184; James, p. 55; Louise Ream, "Heisey Glassware", *GR*, December, 1983, p. 16; Zemel, p. 263 (misidentified).

311. Hammond 1, 1969 edition, p. 123; "From L. E. Smith . . .", *Daze*, May 1, 1982, p. 42; "L. E. Smith", *Daze*, May 1, 1983, p. 44; Reichel 2, p. 56.

312. *WPT 2*, p. 276; Westmoreland advertisements, *CG&L*, February, 1949, p. 1, and *G&AB*, March 1949, p. 40; Ruth Lombardo, "Black Glass", *Daze*, April 1,

1981, p. 8; Frances Bones, "Westmoreland Glass Co.", *Best of GR*, 2, pp. 16, 17; Grace Allison, "Westmoreland Glass", *GR*, December, 1986, pp. 20-22; Virginia Scott, "Looking Through the Ads", *GR*, October, 1981, pp. 34, 35; Barbara Shaeffer, "Summit Art", *GR*, February, 1985, p. 30; Millard, *Opaque Glass*, pl. 236; James, p. 46; Millard, *Goblets*, 2, pl. 106; *LPG*, pp. 503-506 and pls. 137, 146, 158.

313. Ruth Lombardo, "Black Glass", *Daze*, April 1, 1981, p. 8; Westmoreland catalogue, circa 1954, p. 8; Betty E. Bryner in "Glass Review Mailbox", *GR*, October, 1978, p. 29.

314. *W* 2, p. 364.

315. *W* 2, p. 368; Westmoreland catalogue, circa 1967, p. 5; *KG*, 1983 edition, pp. 44, 47.

316. Westmoreland catalogues, circa 1967 (pp. 22, 27), circa 1971 (pp. 16, 19), 1972 supplement (pp. (2, 3)), 1974 supplement (p. 8); *W* 2, p. 378.

317. *W* 2, p. 294; *NM* 2, p. 51; Carolyn Redinger, "Seeking the Elusive Powder Bowl", *Daze*, April 1, 1977, p. 30.

318. Hazel Marie Weatherman, "Picking up the Pieces", Koch 2, p. Weatherman 48; *WPT* 2, p. 273; *W* 2, p. 380; James, p. 78.

319. *W* 2, pp. 364, 373; James, p. 46.

320. Revi, *APGFB*, pp. 322, 335, 341; Ferson, pp. 96, 99, 162, 165; Belknap, pp. 14, 271, 297; Westmoreland catalogue, circa 1954, p. 4; Hammond 1, 1969 edition, p. 133, and 1979 edition, p. 112; Virginia Scott, "Looking Through the Ads", *GR*, January, 1986, pp. 6, 7; Millard, *Opaque Glass*, pl. 21; Lee, *Fakes*, 1950 edition, p. 184; James, p. 66; Batty, p. 250.

321, 322. *W* 2, p. 231.

323. *W* 2, p. 311.

324. *GC* 4, p. 43; *W* 2, p. 111.

331. *W* 2, p. 369; *LVG*, p. 419 and pl. 173.

332. *Bickenheuser 2, p. 121; Millard, Opaque Glass*, pl. 197; *MH* 10, p. 46; *RP* 4, p. 9 and pl. 26; James, p. 63; Stanley, pl. 8.

333. Manley, *Decorative Victorian Glass*, pp. 100, 101 (Figure 338).

334. *NM*, pp. 48, 58; compare date and pattern number in *W* 2, p. 295, and *NM* 2, pp. 17-19.

335. Stout, *DG* 3, pp. 20, 21.

338. Cambridge: Heacock and Johnson, p. 19; "Nearcut", pp. 23, 27, 41, 43, 88, 91; *K* 8, pp. 45, 189; Welker, *Co.* 1, p. 96; *K* 7, pp. 47, 175; Phyllis Smith, "Cambridge Corner", *GR*, February, 1981, p. 19, and April, 1981, p. 32; National Cambridge Collectors, Inc., members of, "'Near Cut' Value Guide No. NC-1", pp. 4, 5, 9; Mark Nye, "Caembridge Corner", *GR*, November, 1985, p. 26, and December, 1986, p. 32. Duncan and Miller: Bones, p. 94; *H* 6, pp. 82, 83; Heacock, *Rare & Unlisted Toothpick Holders*, pp. 42, 84; *H* 7, pp. 41, 199; *K* 2, p. 87; "Duncan's No. 65 Pattern", *National Duncan Glass Journal*, April-June, 1982, pp. 23-25; Heacock, *1000 Toothpick Holders*, pp. 75, 84.

339. Cambridge Glass Company, *1903 Catalog*, p. 106; "*Nearcut*", p. 107; Bones, p. 111; Stout, *McKee*, pp. 132, 134.

340. Imperial Catalog 66A, p. 67; *IG*, p. 120; Reichel 2, p. 29; Heacock and Johnson, pp. 44, 60, 112, 119; James, p. 69; Barbara Shaeffer, "Summit Art", *GR*, February, 1985, p. 28 ("pedestal salt dip" may refer to this item); *W* 2, pp. 159, 160; Hand, pp. 144, 145 (Colonial).

341. Lagerberg 4, Fig. 28; James, p. 63.

342. Measell and Smith, *Findlay Glass*, pp. 98, 110; *CG* 1, pp. 25, 27; McDonald, pp. 37, 39; Smith, *Findlay Pattern Glass*, pp. 63, 110; Thuro 1, p. 253; James, p. 56.

343. Peterson, *Glass Patents and Patterns*, pp. 61, 64; Ferson, p. 137; *MH* 10, p. 34.

344-347. Similar vases: *CG* 2, p. 59; *LVG*, Chapter 21.

348. *LVG*, p. 309 and pl. 110; Belknap, p. 163; Millard, *Opaque Glass*, pl. 310; Ferson, pp. 48, 49; Allison, p. 7; Stanley, pl. 5.

350. Cream jugs of similar shape: Manley, *Decorative Victorian Glass*, pp. 108, 109 (Figure 403); Spillman, p. 368 and pl. 14 (#1426); Batty, pp. 123-125 (#138).

351. Fred Bickenheuser, "Tiffin Glassmasters", *GR*, April 1981, p. 4; letter from Kathe Mattson, *Daze*, July 1980, p. 44.

354. James, p. 73; Heacock, *Rare & Unlisted Toothpick Holders*, p. 67 (bottom row, center, misidentified).

355. Lucas, p. 127; Heacock, *1000 Toothpick Holders*, pp. 32, 57; *CG* 1, p. 48; *CG* 2, p. 6; *LPG*, pl. 180 and p. 622; *LVG*, pls. 89, 201, and pp. 263, 476; Millard, *Opaque Glass*, pl. 199; James, p. 70; Libby Yalom, "Slippers", *GR* September, 1985, p. 15, and March, 1987, pp. 10, 36; "From Mosser Glass Inc . . . .", *Daze*, May 1, 1979, p. 7; Mosser 1982 catalogue, p. 22, and 1983 price list.

356. *GC* 6, p. 17; Millard, *Opaque Glass*, pl. 236; Gaddis, "Keys 2", pl. 8; *H* 4, p. 35; Heacock, *1000 Toothpick Holders*, pp. 31, 35, 57, 62; James, p. 73; Heacock, *Rare & Unlisted Toothpick Holders*, p. 66; *CG* 1, p. 45.

357. Similar bottle: *LVG*, pl. 180.

360. Cambridge Glass Company, *1903 Catalog*, p. 52; Stout, *McKee*, p. 210; *NM* 1, p. 12; *LVG*, p. 396 and pl. 160; Millard, *Opaque Glass*, pl. 197; Stevens, *Early Canadian Glass*, pl. 20 and p. 61; Bennett, p. 63; Stevens, *Glass in Canada*, p. 66; Heacock *1000 Toothpick Holders*, inside front cover and p. 97; Heacock *Rare & Unlisted Toothpick Holders*, p. 62.

364. Forsythe, p. 18 (Figure 134).

368. Bryce Brothers Company, p. 70.

371. Similar items identified as hyacinth glass or vase: Drepperd, p. 49; Stout, *McKee*, p. 87; Gillinder & Sons, Inc., p. 17; *F* 2, p. 92.

375. *W* 2, p. 326.

376. *W* 2, p. 343; United States Glass Company, Duncan and Miller Division catalogue, circa 1957, p. 39; Bickenheuser 3, p. 132; Krause, *Encyclopedia*, p. 88, and Krause, *Years*, p. 171; *MH* 4, pp. 22, 23; *RP* 1, p. 92

and pl. 204; *LVG*, Chapter 4; Millard, *Opaque Glass*, pls. 119, 193; *MH* 9, p. 56.

378. Farrar, *H. P. Sinclaire, Jr., Glassmaker* 2, p. 48.

379. Welker, *Co.* 1, p. 104.

381, 382. Revi, *American Art Nouveau Glass*, p. 164 (Figure 328); Gardner, pl. 24B; Rockwell, p. 18.

383. Bickenheuser 2, p. 150; Welker, *Co.* 1, p. 107; Butler Brothers, *China & Glassware 1925*, p. (16); Warman, *Milk Glass Addenda*, pl. 68 (B).

385. Lafferty, *Fry Insights*, Catalogue No. 10 reprint, p. 18; *Daze*, June 1, 1987, p. 1; *LVG*, pl. 218 and p. 517.

391. *W* 2, p. 305.

394A, B. Stout, *DG* 2, pl. 12 (misidentified).

397. Newlin and Vajner, pp. 5, 6; Betty Newbound, "Along the Flea Market Trail", Koch 1, p. Newbound 28; *W* 2, p. 191.

398A, B. Frances Bones, "Fostoria 'Fairfax'", *Daze*, April 1, 1978, p. 30. *WFG*, pp. 123, 124; *WFP*, pp. 64, 79, 80, 102, 103; James, p. 22.

403. *W* 1, p. 122; *W* 2, p. 114; Stout, *DG* 1, pl. 1.

404. Barnett, pp. 44, 45.

406. *W* 1, pp. 226, 227.

408. James, p. 77.

412. *KG*, 1983 edition, pp. 120, 124, 140, 142, 148, 149.

413. Hazel Marie Weatherman, "Picking up the Pieces", Koch 2, p. Weatherman 48; *WPT* 2, p. 273; Sue Weatherman, "Sue Weatherman On Glassware", *Daze*, December 1, 1981, p. 30.

415. Similar item: *WFG*, p. 243.

417. *W* 2, p. 116; *KG*, 1983 edition, pp. 124, 125.

421. Nora Koch, "Sparkling Clearwater Depression Glass Club's Annual Show & Sale", *Daze*, April 1, 1987, p. 34.

422. Wilson, pp. 121, 158, 178; Innes, pp. 8, 84; Drepperd, pp. 219, 220; McKearin, pp. 183, 189; Stevens. *Glass In Canada*, pp. 56, 57, 62.

423. Rita DeLorme, in Koch 1, p. DeLorme 7; *W* 2, p. 397.

424. *CGC* 2, pp. 244, 245.

426. Pressed pattern: Welker, *Pressed Glass in America*, pp. 322, 323; Thuro 1, pp. 326, 327; Smith, *Findlay Pattern Glass*, pp. 52, 96; *LVG*, pl. 69 and pp. 224, 225; *H* 5, pp. 23, 186; Measell and Smith, *Findlay Glass*, pp. 50, 51; McCain, *Encyclopedia*, pp. 198, 199; *K* 1, p. 64; Lee, *Fakes*, 1950 edition, p. 167; Hammond 2, p. 12; Nora Koch, "My Trip to the Glass and China Companies", *Daze*, May 1980, p. 2; Unitt, *American and Canadian Goblets* 2, p. 211 (shows etching also); McDonald, pp. 41, 59, 93-95; Nora Koch, "Glassroots Research", Koch 2, p. Koch 36 (shows etching also); *H* 1, p. 62 (lists etching also); Batty, p. 248 (lists etching also). Etching: *W* 2, p. 351; Glenita Stearns, "Glancing Back", *GR*, May, 1979, p. 12; *WPT* 2, p. 264; Barnett, p. 44; Butler Brothers, *China & Glassware 1930*, p. (31).

430. *W* 1, pp. 220, 221.

431. *W* 2, p. 171; *IG*, pp. 187, 190, 197.

438. *F* 1, pp. 87, 89.

439. Bickenheuser 2, p. 65.

440. Umbraco, pp. 7, 48, 49.

442. *W* 2, p. 317; Stout, *DPG*, p. 84, and *DG* 1, pl. 16; Glenita Stearns, "Close-Up on Depression Glass", *Best of GR* 2, p. 85.

443. *W* 2, pp. 220, 335.

444. Bickenheuser 1, p. 73.

446A, B, and 447. *WFG*, p. 253; *WFP*, p. 105.

449. James, p. 51.

450. *W* 2, p. 268.

453. Sue Weatherman, "Sue Weatherman On Glassware", *Daze*, November 1, 1981, pp. 7, 11; Blackwell Wielandy Company, p. (19).

454. Stout, *DG* 2, pl. 22; James, p. 50.

456. Robert E. Haltiner, "Bouquets of Glass", *AT Annual* 8, pp. 268-271; letter from Diane Wicklund, "Readers Say", Daze, November 1980, p. 25.

458. Ferson, pp. 113, 114; Eleanor and Howard Lydick, "Historical Glass", *GR*, March, 1982, pp. 33, 34, and November, 1982, p. 28; Reichel 2, pp. 58, 59; Stout, *DG* 3, pp. 20, 21; *F* 2, pp. 51, 58, 130; FAGCA, *Reprints*, items lists for July 1952-January 1952, 1953, 1954, 1955, 1956, 1957, 1958, 1959, 1960, 1961.

459. Belknap, pp. 3, 24.

460. Falker and Stern Company catalogue, Spring, 1898, p. 7; Millard, *Opaque Glass*, pls. 39, 40; Belknap, pp. 271, 278, 298; Westmoreland advertisement; *CG&L*, February, 1949, p. 1; Westmoreland catalogue, 1965, p. 8; Lee, *Fakes*, 1938 edition, p. 151, and 1950 edition, p. 185; Lee, *Fakes Supplement*, p. 31; Hammond 1, 1969 edition, p. 129, and 1979 edition, p. 110; Stout, *DG* 3, pp. 28, 29; Batty, p. 250; Ferson, p. 164; James, p. 64; *LPG*, pp. 368-370 and pls. 115, 121.

461. Lattimore, p. 46 and pl. IV; Godden, p. 69; Notley, pp. 26-28; Raymond Notley, "Sowerby Carnival Glass", *GC*, Spring, 1982, p. 27; *CG* 1, p. 49; Manley, pp. 100-103, 106, 107; Lagerberg 4, Figure 46; William Heacock, "Ruby Colored Glassware", *GC*, Fall, 1982, p. 23.

462. Cambridge Glass Co., *1903 Catalog*, p. 51; *CCG*, pp. 6, 7; Brothers, p. 21; James, p. 64; Batty, pp. 63, 64; Millard, *Opaque Glass*, pl. 45; Belknap, pp. 15, 28; Kemple Glass Works price lists, circa 1952, pp. 6, 8, and 1953; Grace Allison, "Kemple Glass", *GR*, September 1985, pp. 26, 29.

464. Falker and Stern Co. catalogue, Spring, 1898, p. 7; Millard, *Opaque Glass*, pl. 34; Belknap, pp. 19, 22, 23, 26; *LPG*, pls. 44, 164, 189, and pp. 619, 639, 644.

465. Brothers, p. 21; Belknap, pp. 17, 271, 292, 298; Millard, *Opaque Glass*, pl. 10; Westmoreland catalogues, circa 1967 (p. 1), 1974 supplement (p. 4), 1976 supplement (pp. 1, 7, 9), 1977-78 (pp. 2-5, 11, 19, 25-28), circa 1978 brochure (pp. 3, 7), 1979 (pp. 25, 27-31, 35-37), 1980 (pp. 12, 13, 16-18, 22, 23), 1981 (p. 16), 1982 (p. 14); Hammond 1, 1969 edition, p. 129, and 1979 edition, p. 110; Batty, p. 248; "From Westmoreland Glass Company", *Daze*, May 1980, Section

1, p. 21; "Westmoreland Glass Company", *Daze*, May 1, 1983, p. 35, and May 1, 1984, p. 52; Phil and Helen Rosso advertisement, *GR*, May, 1985, inside back cover; James, p. 64.

466. Belknap, p. 19; Millard, *Opaque Glass*, pl. 4.

467. *WPT 2*, pp. 290, 293.

471. *W 2*, p. 309; Jerry Barnett, "The Paden City Glass Mfg. Company", *The Antique Trader Weekly*, April 21, 1982, p. 68; *WPT 2*, pp. 231, 233, 234.

472. Jerry Barnett, "Paden City's White Glass: Opal", *The Paden City Party Line* (Winter, 1981), pp. 6, 7; Jerry Barnett, "Paden City Glass", *GR*, February, 1981, p. 11.

474. Letter from J. R. and letter from A. B., "Readers Say", Koch 1, pp. Readers Say 11, 12; letter from Hildegard Parks and editor's note, "Readers Say", *Daze*, January, 1981, Section 1, p. 4.

475. *The Antique Trader Price Guide to Antiques and Collectors' Items*, October 1984, p. 7; Betty Newbound, "Along the Flea Market Trail", Koch 1, p. Newbound 5.

476. *H 4*, p. 59; *GC*, Summer, 1982, p. 26; Gaddis, "Keys 4", pl. 7.

478. Chinese cameo glass snuff bottles: Munsey, pp. 81-83.

489. Letter from Arline V. Wise, "Readers Say", *Daze*, June 1, 1978, p. 33.

490. *W 2*, p. 246.

491. "Imperial Glass", *GR*, November 1982, p. 38; *W 2*, p. 171.

493. *WFG*, pp. 125, 192, 193, 219, 232, 235, 312; *WFP*, pp. 65, 82, 89, 95, 133, 136.

494. *WFG*, p. 192; *WFP*, pp. 82, 87, 88.

495. Florence, *Akro Agate*, pp. 32, 33; Appleton, pp. 26, 27; Sophia Papapanu, "Powder Jars", Koch 1, p. Papapanu 10.

497. Ruth Lombardo, "Black Glass", *Daze*, March 1, 1981, p. 6; *W 2*, p. 367; Westmoreland catalogues, 1979 (pp. 22, 25, 27, 29, 38), 1980 (pp. 11-14, 20-22), 1981 (pp. 16, 20).

498. Cover: *W 2*, p. 116; *W 1*, pp. 214, 215.

499. "Powder Jars", *Daze*, March 1, 1978, p. 31.

504. Lee, *Fakes Supplement*, p. 67; Lee, *Fakes*, 1950 edition, p. 118; *LPG*, pls. 87, 163, 167, 169, and pp. 588-591.

505. Milbra Long, "Quite a Stir in Dallas", *GR*, May, 1985, p. 16.

506. *NM 2*, p. 49.

520, 521, 524. Appleton, p. 25; Florence, *Akro Agate*, pp. 42, 43; Roni Sionakides, "Jean Vivaudou Co., Inc.", Koch 2, p. Sionakides 8, and "Jean Vivaudou Co., Inc. Part 2", *Daze*, April 1, 1977, p. 28, and "J. Vivaudou Company", *Daze*, April 1980, p. 41.

523. Milbra Long, "Quite a Stir in Dallas", *GR*, May, 1985, p. 16.

533. *CG 3*, p. 11; William Heacock in *GC*, Summer, 1982, front cover and inside front cover.

535. Sophia Papapanu, "Houze Rocker Blotters", *Daze*, December 1, 1977, pp. 1, 36; William Heacock, "A Study in Jade and Black", *GC*, Spring-Summer, 1983, pp. 29, 36; letter from B. H., "Readers Say", Koch 1, p. Readers Say 46.

543. Pattern name: *LPG*, Chapter 11.

544. Munsey, p. 98; Belknap, p. 259; Ferson, pp. 85, 87.

545. *W 2*, p. 20 (shows font and base separately).

546. *W 2*, p. 398.

551. Similar item: *W 2*, p. 255.

554. William Heacock, "A Study in Jade and Black", *GC*, Spring-Summer, 1983, pp. 26-29.

555. Avila, pp. 91, 141.

557-559. Decoration: Fenton advertisement, *GR*, December 1982, p. 48; "Items Discontinued From the Fenton Catalog as of January 1, 1983", *Butterfly Net*, November 1982, p. 14; Gwen Shumpert, "Gwen's Glassline", *GR*, December, 1986, pp. 14, 16. Figure 557 shape: Fenton catalogue, 1981-1982, pp. 50, 51, and supplement, January 1982, p. 19; Ruth Lombardo, "Black Glass", *Daze*, May 1981, Section 1, p. 8; "Fenton Art Glass Company", *Daze*, May 1, 1982, p. 69; Fenton advertisements, *GR*, June, 1982, back cover, and December, 1982, p. 48; "Items Discontinued From the Fenton Catalog as of June 1, 1982", *Butterfly Net*, June 1982, p. 9; "Items Discontinued From the Fenton Catalog as of January 1, 1983", *Butterfly Net*, November 1982, pp. 13, 14; Gwen Shumpert, "Gwen's Glassline", *GR*, December, 1986, pp. 14, 16. Figure 558 shape: Fenton Catalog Supplement, January 1982, pp. 1, 3, 16, 17; Fenton advertisements, *GR*, January-February, 1982, back cover, and December, 1982, p. 48; "Fenton Art Glass Company", *Daze*, May 1, 1982, p. 69; "Items Discontinued From the Fenton Catalog as of January 1, 1983", *Butterfly Net*, November 1982, p. 14. Figure 559 shape: Fenton Catalog Supplement, January 1982, pp. 3, 16; Fenton advertisement, *GR*, January-February, 1982, back cover; "Items Discontinued From the Fenton Catalog as of June 1, 1982", *Butterfly Net*, June 1982, p. 9; "Items Discontinued From the Fenton Catalog as of January 1, 1983", *Butterfly Net*, November 1982, p. 14.

560. Fenton advertisement, Supplement to *Gift & Tableware Reporter*, first issue August, 1970; William Heacock, "A Glass Door Stop???", *GC*, Summer, 1982, p. 35; Bickenheuser 2, pp. 116, 133; Mary Van Pelt, "Fantastic Figurines", *GR*, December, 1977, pp. 12, 13; Fred Bickenheuser, "The Tiffin Glassmasters", *GR*, December, 1979, pp. 22, 23; James, p. 43; Reichel 1, p. 9; Gwen Shumpert, "Gwen's Glassline", *Best of GR 3*, pp. 85, 86, and *GR*, April, 1987, p. 16; Levay Distributing Company advertisements, *Butterfly Net*, March 1980, and *GR*, February, 1985, p. 43; Taylor, pp. 3, 4.

562. Linn, pl. 9; James, p. 18.

563. Fenton Catalog Supplements, January 1980 (pp. 10, 12, 16) and June 1980 (p. 8), and catalogues, 1981-1982, pp. 23, 27, 29, and 1983-84, p. 4; "From Fenton Glass Co.", *Daze*, May 1980, Section 1, p. 7; "Items Discontinued From the Fenton Catalog as of January 1, 1982", *Butterfly Net*, January 1982, p. 14;

Items Discontinued From the Fenton Catalog as of January 1, 1984", *Butterfly Net*, November 1983, p. 12.

564. FAGCA, *Reprints*, for 1962 (items list and one color page), 1963 (items list), 1964 (items list and one color page), 1965 (items list), and 1966 (items list); Fenton 1963 catalogue, p. 19, and July 1963 supplement, p. (2); Roserita Ziegler, "Researching With Roserita", *GR*, May, 1982, p. 35, and June, 1982, p. 40; Linn, pl. 10; "Thumbprint", *Butterfly Net*, July 1985, p. 5.

565. Gail Krause, "Delightfully Duncan", *GR*, March, 1982, p. 11; Ferill J. Rice, "Happiness Is Fenton Glass", *Daze*, November 1, 1983, p. 10; Fenton catalogues, 1977-78 (pp. 1, 33, 40, 57, 63, 65, 67, 69, 72), 1979-1980 (pp. 28, 31, 35, 37, 38), and January 1980 supplement (pp. 10, 13); "From Fenton Glass Co.", *Daze*, May 1980, Section 1, p. 8; Fenton catalogues, June 1980 supplement (back cover), 1981-1982 (pp. 11, 23, 27, 29, 71), 1983-84 (pp. 4, 32), and January 1984 supplement (p. 2); James, p. 18; *Butterfly Net*, December 1978 ("Items to Be Discontinued", p. 8), January 1982 ("Items Discontinued From the Fenton Catalog as of January 1, 1982", p. 14), November 1982 ("Items Discontinued From the Fenton Catalog as of January 1, 1983", p. 14), and November 1984 ("Discontinued", p. 11).

566. Fenton 1963 catalogue, p. 19, and July, 1963 supplement, p. (2); Linn, pl. 9; "Thumbprint", *Butterfly Net*, July 1985, p. 6; "Gift Shop Display in 1968 Ebony Crest and Black Items", *Butterfly Net*, March 1983, p. 9; Ferill J. Rice, "Happiness Is Fenton Glass", *Daze*, October, 1, 1986, p. 40; FAGCA, *Reprints*, items lists for 1963, 1964, 1965, and 1966; *LPG*, pp. 182-186 and pls. 15, 17, 18, 24, 59.

567A, B, C. Betty Newbound, "Along the Flea Market Trail", *Daze*, April 1, 1983, p. 42 (567B decoration); Westmoreland catalogues, circa 1954 (p. 8, 567A, B, and C decorations), circa 1967 (p. 23, 567A, B, and C decorations), circa 1971 (p. 8, 567A and C decorations), 1977-78 (p. 29), 1979 (p. 28), 1980 (p. 18), 1981 (pp. 1, 23); Hammond 1, 1969 edition, pp. 129, 144 (567 A, B, and C decorations), and 1979 edition, pp. 110, 120 (567A, B and C decorations); Spillman, p. 356 (567C decoration); Belknap, pp. 20 (pl. 16a, possibly Westmoreland's), 271, 277, 289, 298; "Where Are the Molds?", *GR*, May, 1985, p. 33; Lafferty, *The Forties Revisited* 1, p. 61 (567B decoration), and *The Forties Revisited* 2, front cover; James, pp. 66-68; Millard, *Opaque Glass*, pls. 3, 8, 26; Brothers, p. 21; Cambridge Glass Company, *1903 Catalog*, p. 50; Ferson, p. 165; Lee, *Fakes*, 1938 edition, pl. 65 and p. 151, and 1950 edition, pl. 93 and p. 185.

572. Westmoreland catalogues, 1965 (p. 7), circa 1967, pp. 11, 23, and circa 1971, p. 16; Hammond 1, 1969 edition, p. 140, and 1979 edition, p. 116; *W* 2, p. 378.

573. Ruth Lombardo, "Black Glass", *Daze*, March 1, 1981, p. 6; Westmoreland catalogues, 1981, pp. 20, 25, 27, and 1982, pp. 22-25, 28; "From Westmoreland Glass Company", *Daze*, May 1981, Section 1, p. 29.

574. *K* 3, p. 74 and pl. 3; *OPG*, p. 42; *H* 5, pp. 16, 47, 64, 72; *H* 3, p. 83; Revi, *APGFB*, pp. 18, 19; *LVG*, pl. 48 and pp. 140, 141; *H* 7, pp. 31, 92, 97; Belknap, p. 286; Westmoreland catalogues, circa 1954 (pp. 3, 7), 1965

(pp. 35, 39), circa 1967 (pp. 1, 5, 13, 17), circa 1971 (pp. 1, 2, 4), 1976 supplement (pp. 1, 9), 1977-78 (pp. 1, 10, 11, 19, 24, 26, 27), 1979 (pp. 26, 29), 1980 (front cover, inside front cover, and p. 11), 1981 (pp. 18, 19), and 1982 (p. 16); Hammond 1, 1969 edition, pp. 74, 136, 138, and 1979 edition, pp. 70, 114, 122; Bev Wantin, "A History of Westmoreland", Koch 2, p. Wantin 16; "Westmoreland Glass Company", *Daze*, May 1, 1984, p. 53; Lee, *Fakes*, 1950 edition, pl. 85 and pp. 148, 164; United States Glass Company, Duncan and Miller Division, catalogue, circa 1957, p. 38; Bickenheuser 3, p. 132; Krause, *Encyclopedia*, p. 88, and *Years*, p. 171; *W* 2, p. 207; "From Jeannette Glass Co. . . .", *Daze*, May 1, 1979, p. 40, and May, 1981, Section 1, p. 25; Nora Koch, "Jeannette Glass Company", *Daze*, November 1, 1985, p. 60; Millard, *Goblets* 2, pl. 43; *K* 8, p. 58 and pls. 12, 13; Innes, pp. 51, 380, 381, 433, 434.

575. *W* 2, p. 378; Westmoreland catalogues, 1965 (p. 7), circa 1967 (pp. 11, 22, 23, 27), and 1971 (pp. 16, 18); *Candlesticks*, pp. 173, 174.

576. Westmoreland catalogues, 1976 supplement (pp. 2, 7, 8), 1977-78 (p. 31), 1979 (p. 38), 1980 (p. 36), and 1981 (p. 38); "From Westmoreland Glass Company", *Daze*, May 1980, Section 1, p. 21.

577. *W* 2, p. 369; Westmoreland catalogues, 1971 (pp. 2, 11, 17, 19), 1974 supplement (pp. 3, 4), 1976 supplement (pp. 1, 3, 7, 9), 1977-78 (pp. 2-9, 11, 19, 28, 29), circa 1978 brochure (pp. 1-3, 6), 1979 (pp. 25, 27, 28, 30, 31, 37, 38), 1980 (pp. 12-14, 18, 22-24, and inside back cover), 1981 (pp. 15, 16, 20, 35), and 1982 (pp. 14, 20, 21, 25); "From Westmoreland Glass Company", *Daze*, May 1980, Section 1, p. 21, and May 1981, Section 1, p. 29; "Westmoreland Glass Company", *Daze*, May 1, 1983, p. 35, and May 1, 1984, p. 52.

578. Westmoreland catalogues, circa 1971 (p. 6) and 1980 (p. 36); "From Westmoreland Glass Company", *Daze*, May 1980, Section 1, p. 21.

579. Belknap, pp. 273, 274, 294; Westmoreland catalogues, circa 1954 (p. 2), 1965 (p. 19), circa 1967 (p. 12), circa 1971 (p. 6), 1980 (p. 36), and 1980 folder; Nora Koch, "Westmoreland", Koch 2, p. Koch 34; "From Westmoreland Glass Company", *Daze*, May 1980, Section 1, pp. 20, 21; Hammond 1, 1969 edition, p. 145, and 1979 edition, p. 121; "Who Bought the Westmoreland Molds?", *GR*, April, 1985, p. 10; *GR*, May, 1987, p. 32.

580. Westmoreland catalogues, 1965 (pp. 18, 38), circa 1967 (pp. 6, 13, 15, 17), circa 1971 (p. 12), 1974 supplement (pp. 2, 8), 1976 supplement (p. 3), 1977-78 (pp. 24, 26, 27, 30), 1979 (pp. 19, 23), 1980 (pp. 15, 28), and 1981 (p. 29); Betty Newbound, "Along the Flea Market Trail", *Daze*, June 1, 1979, p. 43; Hammond 1, 1969 edition, p. 136, and 1979 edition, p. 122.

581. Westmoreland catalogues, circa 1954 (p. 2), 1965 (p. 32), circa 1967 (pp. 8, 14, 15), circa 1971 (pp. 2, 14), 1974 supplement (p. 2), 1977-78 catalogue (pp. 24, 26, 27), 1979 (pp. 10, 19, 23), 1980 (pp. 11, 15, 28), and 1981 (p. 29); Betty Newbound, "Along the Flea Market Trail", *Daze*, June 1, 1979, p. 43; Hammond 1, 1969 edition, p. 136, and 1979 edition, p. 122.

582. Westmoreland catalogues, 1980, (p. 19), 1981 (p. 14), and 1982 (pp. 11, 30); "Westmoreland Glass

Company", *Daze*, May 1, 1984, p. 52.

583. *W* 2, p. 369; Ruth Lombardo, "Black Glass", *Daze*, April 1, 1981, p. 8; Westmoreland catalogues, 1967 (p. 12), circa 1971 (p. 7), 1976 supplement (p. 8), and 1977-78 (p. 33); Zemel, p. 276; "Who Bought the Westmoreland Molds?", *GR*, April, 1985, p. 10; *GR*, May, 1987, p. 32; *WPT2*, 1977 edition, p. 5; *F 1*, p. 113; Mary Van Pelt, "Fantastic Figurines", *GR*, March, 1977, p. 23; James, p. 59.

584, 585. Newlin and Vajner, pp. 3-5, 7, 8, 12, 13, 15, 16.

586. Newlin and Vajner, pp. 5, 6.

587. "Indiana Glass Company", *Daze*, May, 1981, Section 1, p. 37; Newlin and Vajner, pp. 3, 4.

588. Newlin and Vajner, pp. 5, 6.

590. Newlin and Vajner, p. 3.

591. Newlin and Vajner, pp. 5, 6.

592. Newlin and Vajner, pp. 5, 6; Koch 1, p. Newbound 28; *W* 2, pp. 190, 191; Bond, p. 106; *W* 1, pp. 127, 196, 197; Stout, *DG* 2, pl. 16.

593. "Tiara Exclusives", *Daze*, May 1, 1982 (p. 32), May 1, 1984 (p. 43), May 1, 1985 (p. 30), May 1, 1986 (p. 41), and May 1, 1987 (p. 41); Newlin and Vajner, pp. 5, 6; "Federal Glass Company A Giant Is Dead", *Daze*, August 1, 1979, p. 40.

594. Newlin and Vajner, pp. 5, 6; Nora Koch, "Indiana Glass Company", Koch 2, p. Koch 29; "From Indiana Glass Company . . . .", *Daze*, May 1980, Section 1, p. 11; "Indiana Glass Company", *Daze*, May 1981, Section 1 (p. 37), May 1, 1984 (p. 44), May 1, 1985 (p. 30), May 1, 1986, p. 40, and May 1, 1987, p. 40; Revi, *Nineteenth Century Glass*, pp. 135 ff.; *LVG*, pp. 102, 103, 245, and pls. 36, 76; Belknap, pp. 226, 233; *K 7*, p. 68; *K 8*, p. 138; Welker, *Pressed Glass in America*, p. 333; *OPG*, pp. 6, 7; *W* , pp. 48-51; *LPG*, pp. 135-138 and pls. 42-45.

595. Newlin and Vajner, pp. 5, 6.

596. Bond, p. 85; "From Indiana Glass Company . . . .", *Daze*, May 1980, Section 1, p. 9; Newlin and Vajner, pp. 5, 6; Reichel 2, p. 43; Millard 2, pl. 116 and index; Taylor, p. 75.

597. "Tiara Exclusives", *Daze*, May 1, 1982, p. 32, and May 1, 1984, p. 42; Newlin and Vajner, pp. 3, 5, 7, 8, 15, 16.

598. "Tiara Exclusives", *Daze*, May 1, 1982, p. 32, and May 1, 1984, p. 43; Newlin and Vajner, pp. 2, 3, 13, 15, 16.

599, 600. Lee, *Fakes*, 1950 edition, pl. 97 and p. 183; Hammond 1, 1969 edition, p. 71, and 1979 edition, p. 67; "Jennings Red Barn", *Daze*, May 1981, Section 1, p. 19; Belknap, pp. 157, 273, 274; Ferson, pp. 14, 15, 166, 167; McGrain, p. 58.

601. Appleton, pp. 12, 13, 34, 35; Joseph A. A. Bourque, "Variegated Akro", *Daze*, May 1, 1977, pp. 32, 33; Florence, *Akro Agate*, pp. 34, 35; Sophia Papapanu, "Akro Agate", Koch 1, pp. Papapanu 19, 21, 22.

602. Westmoreland catalogues, circa 1967 (pp. 12, 24, 27), circa 1971 (pp. 7, 19), 1977-78 (inside back cover), 1979 (p. 24 and inside back cover), 1980 (p. 35), 1982 (p. 26); Hammond 1, 1969 edition, p. 127, and 1979 edition, p. 109; Nora Koch, "Glass Roots Research", Koch 2, p. Koch 34; "From Westmoreland Glass Company", *Daze*, May 1980, Section 1, pp. 20, 21, and May, 1981, Section 1, p. 29; "Westmoreland Glass Company", *Daze*, May 1, 1982, p. 44; Keith and Uni Marbutt, "Jade-ite", *GR*, March, 1987, p. 20.

603. Mosser *New Items 1983 Price Sheet Retail* and illustrated sheet supplementing 1982 catalogue.

604. Boyd's advertisements, *GR*, November, 1982 (p. 64), December, 1982 (p. 48 and inside back cover), March, 1983 (p. 64 and inside back cover), April, 1983 (p. 48 and inside back cover), May, 1983 (p. 64 and inside back cover), June, 1983 (p. 64), September, 1983 (p. 48), November, 1983 (p. 48 and inside back cover), December, 1983 (p. 48), January/February, 1984 (inside back cover), May, 1984 (p. 48), July/August, 1984 (p. 48 and inside back cover), September, 1984 (p. 48 and inside back cover), October, 1984 (p. 48), November, 1984, (p. 48), January, 1985 (p. 48), and March, 1985 (p. 48 and inside back cover).

605. Mosser 1982 catalogue, p. 25, and 1983 price list.

606. Florence, *Degenhart*, pp. 24, 36, 37; Tarter, p. 4; Boyd advertisements, *GR* (inside back cover except as noted), January, March (p. 60), and April, 1979, May, June, August, September, October, and November, 1980, February (p. 64), May (p. 64), and October (also p. 88), November (p. 84), and December (p. 64), 1981, September (p. 64) and December (p. 64), 1982, March (also p. 64), April (also p. 48), May (also p. 64), June (p. 64), September (also p. 48), October (p. 48), November (p. 48), and December (p. 48), 1983, January/February, March (p. 48), April (p. 48), and July/August (also p. 48), 1984, January (also p. 48) and March (also p. 48), 1985, and July, 1986, p. 45; "From Crystal Art Glass", *Daze*, May, 1980, p. 4; "From Boyd's Crystal Art Glass", *Daze*, May 1981, Section 1, p. 38; Heacock and Johnson, pp. 62, 63, 120; *W* 2, p. 368; Westmoreland catalogues, circa 1954 (p. 2), circa 1967 (p. 12), circa 1971 (p. 6), 1977-78 (inside back cover); Belknap, pp. 274, 294; Hammond 1, 1969 edition, p. 145, and 1979 edition, p. 121; Zemel, p. 281.

607. Tarter, pp. 5, 11, 12; "Degenhart Update"; Florence, *Degenhart*, pp. 21, 40, 41; Boyd advertisements, *GR* (inside back cover except as noted), April, June, and December, 1979, May, July, and October, 1980, February (p. 64), May (also p. 64), and December (p. 96), 1981, May (p. 62), November (p. 64), and December (p. 64), 1982, March (also p. 64) and June (p. 64), 1983, March (p. 48), May (p. 48), September (p. 48), and October (p. 48), 1984; "On Exhibit", *GR*, April, 1985, p. 25; "From Crystal Art Glass", *Daze*, May 1980, Section 1, p. 4; "From Boyd's Crystal Art Glass . . .", *Daze*, May 1981, Section 1, p. 38; Ferson, pp. 22, 23, 152, 156, 157; Belknap, pp. 186, 274, 275; Kemple price lists, circa 1952, p. 5, and 1953; Batty, p. 250; Hammond 1, 1969 edition, p. 71, and 1979 edition, p. 67; "Jennings Red Barn", *Daze*, May 1981, Section 1, p. 19.

614. Mosser 1982 catalogue, pp. 2, 8, 24.

615. Mosser 1982 catalogue, pp. 2, 8, 24.

622. Sandy Jenkins, "New Glassmakers and Their Logos", *GR*, October, 1982, p. 36; Guernsey advertisement, *GR*, November, 1981, p. 78.

623. Sandy Jenkins, "New Glassmakers and Their Logos," *GR*, October 1982, p. 36; Guernsey advertisement, *GR*, November 1981, p. 78.

625. Sandy Jenkins, "New Glassmakers and Their Logos", *GR*, October, 1982, p. 36.

626. Jenkins, "New Glassmakers and Their Logos," *GR*, October 1982, p. 36.

627. Mirror Images advertisement, *GR*, July-August 1981, p. 83.

628. Our Gang advertisement, *GR*, November 1981, p. 56.

629. J & B advertisement, *GR*, July-August 1981, p. 76; Botson advertisement, *GR*, March 1984, p. 46.

631. Mosser 1982 catalogue.

632. Botson advertisement, *GR*, March 1984, p. 46.

633. Heacock, *1000 Toothpick Holders*, pp. 33, 34, 58-60.

634. Heacock, *1000 Toothpick Holders*, pp. 33, 34, 58-60.

635. Craig advertisement, *GR*, November 1980, p. 74; Botson advertisement, *GR*, March 1984, p. 46.

636. *GR*, November 1981, cover and p. 3; Botson advertisement, *GR*, March 1984, p. 46; Newbound, p. 23.

641. Boyd advertisements, *GR*, May 1979, inside back cover, and January-February 1983, p. 64.

642. Florence, *Degenhart*, pp. 22, 78, 79, 94, 95.

643. Florence, *Degenhart*, pp. 22, 78, 79, 94, 95.

644. Mosser 1982 catalogue, p. 19.

646. Heacock and Johnson, pp. 27, 106.

647. Heacock and Johnson, pp. 27, 106.

265. *W* 2, pp. 321, 322; Weatherman, "Hazel Weatherman on Depression Glass", Koch 1, p. Weatherman 13; Belknap, p. 265.